Connie Jakab is honest. In this book, she's honest with herself and with you, and she points to the culture around us and calls it what it is: empty. Will you accept her challenge to rebel against this emptiness and choose to live for what really matters? To be a rebel with a cause?
—Amy Simpson Editor, GiftedForLeadership.com

Culture Rebel, is refreshing, engaging, motivating and honest. Yes, an honest look at life, at our values that control us. It puts the mirror right in our faces and helps us to stop pretending and start doing something worthwhile with our lives. Tired of the ordinary, needing new impetus to make your world better? Culture Rebel will get you on the path.
—Ian Green, executive director of Proton Foundation,
www.protonfoundation.com

Grab a homemade coffee and put on your comfy-pants before sitting down to read this book. In Culture Rebel, *Connie takes you on a journey away from the status quo and into the world of dissatisfaction with what is normal. It's not a particularly easy process, but the move from status quo to culture rebel and then on to culture-maker is the only option when we get a grasp for the heart of God. Read this book and your world just might change!*
—Jeremy Postal, missional leader of Whistler, BC

If you are happy with being a "success-crazed, comfort-seeking, status-hungry consumer," then you better watch out: Connie Jakab has some strong words for you. But if you struggle with the temptation to be that kind of person and you desire instead to live a life of purpose and meaning, then read Culture Rebel, *because Connie Jakab has some strong words for you. This bold, honest, spirited book will challenge you toward a life that more deeply resembles the greatest culture rebel of all—Jesus—who knew a few things about saying strong words. Connie's words may not always be easy to read as they target those areas in your life that need stretching. But go with the stretching, and be prepared to be transformed into a culture rebel yourself.*

—Helen Lee, author of *The Missional Mom*
and founding member of Redbud Writers Guild

Culture Rebel *is like sitting down with Connie Jakab over a cup of coffee and having her passionately share the insights that come to a young women who is determined to seriously follow Jesus and impact her world. Engage in the conversation and be encouraged to be the culture rebel Jesus calls us to be.*

—Dave Wells, *superintendent of the Pentecostal Assemblies of Canada*

This book is fierce; it's fiery and will inspire you to change your life for the greater good! I believe it will challenge and redefine culture as we know it. Culture rebel will become a new term in the dictionary, and Connie has effectively and powerfully described what it takes for people to go from being part of a society that continues to dominate our "consumer" mindsets to becoming an ultimate culture rebel and being who we are really meant to be. This account is personal, refreshing, and will encourage you to be BRAVE and really LIVE your life to the fullest!

—Marika, recording artist

CULTURE REBEL

Because the world has enough desperate housewives

Connie Jakab

WestBow
PRESS
A DIVISION OF THOMAS NELSON

WestBow Press books may be ordered through booksellers or by contacting:

WestBow Press
A Division of Thomas Nelson
1663 Liberty Drive
Bloomington, IN 47403
www.westbowpress.com
1-(866) 928-1240

Because of the dynamic nature of the Internet, any web addresses or links contained in this book may have changed since publication and may no longer be valid. The views expressed in this work are solely those of the author and do not necessarily reflect the views of the publisher, and the publisher hereby disclaims any responsibility for them.

Any people depicted in stock imagery provided by Thinkstock are models, and such images are being used for illustrative purposes only.

Certain stock imagery © Thinkstock.

ISBN: 978-1-4497-5738-0 (sc)
ISBN: 978-1-4497-5737-3 (e)

Library of Congress Control Number: 2012912853

Printed in the United States of America

WestBow Press rev. date: 08/02/2012

To my husband for being brave enough to marry a culture rebel and for supporting yet another crazy idea.

TABLE OF CONTENTS

Why I Wrote This Book

I like to live on the edge. I'm a brave, gutsy, ADD type of gal who can't sit still. The problem is that I've lived on the wrong edge for the last twenty years. Since my first full-time job, I have lived a life with *me* at the center of my attention, and now I have nothing to show for all my years of work, college, and career. Coming close to forty, this has caused much introspection. What I'm discovering isn't nice to look at.

Ask me how much I've saved in twenty years? Zip. Well, that's not entirely true. Thank goodness I have a savvy hubby who saves money in places I wouldn't want to mention for fear of making you blush. So yes, I have some savings … through him.

Even more pressing, ask me how much I've given in twenty years? Okay, that I can brag about a bit; I love to give. I consider myself to be pretty generous. I love taking people out and giving lovely gifts; it's nothing, really. I just put it on this shiny silver card that I carry in my wallet, and I don't feel a thing. The problem with this shiny card is that they send letters to my hubby, and he's never in a good mood after he opens their mail. What's that about?

Ask me where I'm sitting right now writing this book. Starbucks, but isn't that where all the cool writers write? Yup, I'm pretty trendy sitting here with my five-dollar coffee that's already cold. I think I must own stock in this place. Oh, no, I don't mean their bean stock, which I've heard great things about. I've decided to go a more modest route: If I buy one five-dollar coffee per day, let's see— I'm not so great at math, but that's got to be around 1,625 dollars a year. (Pretty impressive "estimate," eh?) Okay, I totally used my calculator, but getting back to my "investment," with all that five-dollar coffee inside me, I should be heading toward becoming a part owner of this place one day! Or maybe not ...

Are you wondering where else all my money has gone in the last twenty years? Me too, but I have some ideas. I love movies. Actually, I really just like the popcorn; the movie is an added bonus. I also love clothes ... and "bling." Not Tiffany's "bling," but "bling" nonetheless. I'm not a show off, but I really like those big rhinestone earrings that hit the shoulder (from their great length) and make my head go lopsided when I've put one in one ear. I've lost my wedding ring ... twice. I've owned some great clothing too, but I don't know where half of it has gone. I did see one of my items in a local Salvation Army store, and I almost bought it again; it was beautiful!

I'm not a "shoe person." I don't fully understand those people. I mean, what a waste of money. Not to mention, what a clutter nightmare! Don't get me wrong. I do own a pair of heels that I bought in three different colors to be sure that I could match all the basic wardrobe essentials. I have boots with both heels and without (because sometimes you just don't want to wear heels while you are grocery shopping), and each of these are in three different colors. But that's all just practical, isn't it? I have runners for dance (naturally in every color to match my hip-hop Adidas jackets). And of course, I purchase new runners every six months for running because I don't want to injure my coming-up-to-midlife knees! Nope, I'm definitely not a shoe person; I think I'm more of a coat person. Now *that* makes more sense to me. I have a coat in every shape, color, size, and style you can imagine—leather, tweed, fleece, down. I consider this shopping addiction more practical, as I live in a winter city. Keep warm *and* stylish. Win-win.

I'm also a sucker for diet books and trends; if there's a diet book out there, I own it. I'm considering opening my own library in my basement. Name a diet-fad product, and I'm sure I've tried it: pills, shakes, bars, metabolism-boosting drinks, and stretch-mark cream (what a farce!). I've done every diet program out there: Jenny Craig, Weight Watchers, raw food, vegan, drink-nothing-but-soup (I passed out on that one), Eat Clean, Balkan, and fitness model. (On that last one, I got to put chocolate pudding powder in my protein shakes! What a treat!) Then there's all the equipment I've purchased. (Old exercise equipment make lovely side tables, by the way). There's the BOSU, the band, kettlebells, a treadmill, the yoga block, a medicine ball, a bender ball, a pilates ball (really anything that ends with "ball"). And I can't forget to mention my workout DVD library, which consists of Jillian Michaels, Windsor Pilates, yoga (every type just to cover all my bases), Hip-Hop Abs, P90X, and Richard Simmons. Did I just say Richard Simmons? Geesh, how did that get in there? Who has *that* one, right?

I should probably just make a quick note about my love for my hair; it's my crown, and I love doing funky things to it. There's nothing like a trip to the hair salon! I *have* to dye my hair. No, really, I do; you should see how many gray hairs I have! I even have them in my eyebrows, which also calls for a trip to the spa to get my brows plucked and waxed. Maybe add a manicure onto my bill while you're at it. Add a pedicure for ten dollars? What a great deal! Twist my rubber arm!

Last thing, I promise. Mascara. I have yet to find the one that gives me the lashes that Drew Barrymore has on the commercials. One day, I will find my dream mascara. It's a long-term goal that I have. Wow, I think that's it—

Yes, as you can see, I've made a huge investment in a product called "me." It's the edge I've lived on the last twenty years. It's the edge that keeps me thinking that a new shirt, a night out, a manicure, a new diet, and a Starbucks will give me the life I've always wanted. I will be hot. I will be sexy. I will have the respect of everyone around me. That's what the advertisement said just before it said, "I'm worth it."

Yet I'm discovering that this "edge" really isn't an edge at all. It has become dull and unfulfilling. I've given it a real "go" for a while now. It keeps promising me "babe" status, but I find I have to keep going back for refills. I'm sick of it. My hubby's sick of it. Actually, I think he's sicker of those letters he keeps getting from this strange person named "Visa." Maybe you relate?

A self-centered existence leaves us with a life without purpose. I have found a new edge that I'm dying to tell you about. That's what this book is about. I want to share my journey with you in the hopes that you may also find the strength to make the shift to a more altruistic, adventurous life filled with the purpose you were born to find. It's not about money or stuff but a way of living that in some strange way delivers the promise that all of the stuff I just mentioned tried to promise but couldn't deliver. It's called being a culture rebel. What does this look like? Let's find out.

Rebel without a Cause

I love the thought of being a rebel. I've always been one to go against the flow. And what's life without a bit of mischief? Like the time in college we used to put laundry detergent in the fountain downtown—but that's another story. I'm not talking about pranks or rebelling against authority. I'm talking about rebelling against what our culture tells us is "normal."

Here's the problem: too many adults are living with absolutely no purpose, and they are raising their kids and teens to follow in their no-purpose footsteps. That doesn't mean these adults are not looking for purpose in their lives. Every day, we all actively search for it and find it in things our culture tells us we will find it in: status, success, wealth, beauty, intelligence, innovation, comfort, the good life, stocks, retirement, and beer. (That last example is random, but who doesn't want a nice cold one after looking at the foam falling down the glass on the commercial? And I don't even like beer!)

The truth is that you will become whatever you're investing your mental, physical, and monetary energies in. Before you think you're going to turn into a stick of mascara, let me clarify. If my thoughts, actions, and money are spent on trying to stay forever twenty-one, then that's what I'll become. Wait! Sweet! Oh, I fell for it again, didn't I? That's what they want you to believe, but the reality is that you're a hamster in a wheel. One day, that mascara will run out. You'll need more. But not the one you have; you'll need the new one. You know, the brand you saw on the commercial while you were watching *American Idol*. Cover Girl has created mascara with the new technology of microfibers that make you look as if you have false eyelashes! You run out to buy it because your mind is consumed with the luscious-lash status you need to maintain. This new mascara will complete your package. It doesn't matter that it's midnight. The drug store is conveniently open for just this kind of makeup emergency … and the odd person who is desperately ill and in need of a pharmacy. But let's get back to what's important, namely the mascara.

The problem is that it doesn't end with mascara. You'll do anything to be beautiful, won't you? New makeup, clothes, a sexy personal trainer, a facial, maybe some Botox—all to try to feel good. It may be to keep your status or perhaps gain some. It may be to get the job, get the man, get your friend's man, become the alpha, or stick it to the bullies who used to call you fat. Many of us would just settle for escaping the post-baby "frump."

We're victims of today's culture that screams, "You can look like this," and, "You'll feel like this!" While we stand in line at Walmart, we see this cultural message through the smiling celebrity who is staring at us from the cover of a magazine. What we don't know is that they put the poor girl on the nothing-but-chicken-and-broccoli-every-three-hours diet from hell and deprived her of water twenty-four hours before the photo shoot so that her bicep would curve just the way you see it, and as she almost fainted, she had enough composure to smile for the camera. What we also don't see is that just after the click of the camera, she was rushed by ambulance to the hospital while the magazine quickly edited, airbrushed, and stuck her photo on the cover for you and me to see. Sigh. I want to look just like her.

Okay, maybe she didn't faint, but we all know the truth, don't we? We know that what we see on the magazine cover isn't fully real, yet we still fall for it. It's because we live in poverty—poverty of the soul. Western culture has defined the reality around us and has left us depleted of all meaning. We're calloused, disillusioned, and broken. "People living in today's Western society—thought to have everything—are overindulged and over-entertained and yet are often the most depressed, bored, anxious generation of all time" (Alan Hirsch, *Untamed*).

What does popular culture tell us? It tells us that it's normal to do what's best for us. It tells us that we should satisfy our desires. You deserve a break today. Go get another Kit Kat candy bar. Rough day? Find your "happy place" in a Starbucks latte. You need a new outfit. Those are last year's colors. Your vehicle is getting old, and there's a sale on last year's BMWs. Buy two and don't pay till 2025! What a deal!

We are taught to get in with the right people to get us where we want to go. It's not what you know. It's who you know. In Matthew Barnett's book *The Cause within You*, he describes this state. "What we wind up with is a society in which every person sees others either as competition or obstacles rather than recipients to be served. People become commodities that are simply a means through which we gain satisfaction." Ouch.

I'm going to step out on a limb, swallow a bit of humble pie, and admit that often my new outfit and new hairstyle is not just *me* trying to make *me* feel good. That's part of my motivation, for sure. It's what I'll tell you, but inside, my new outfit and my new hairstyle are attempts to become the focus of the room, to maintain the status I've worked hard for. To make people think, "Geesh, that girl's got it going on." I want you to think that I've got it all together. If my makeup can stay unsmudged, and my hair can look ready for a Pantene commercial, all while I walk in heels without stumbling (with my two perfect children dressed like Gap models), then I've succeeded. If I can get other people to think just as a quick passing thought, "Wow, Connie really has everything together in her life. Wish I were like her," I've just won.

Some of you relate to my actions. Others can't imagine thinking like that. You are the type my kind targets for control. Some of you are smarter than that and continue to march to the beat of your own drum. I like you. I find myself thinking, "Wow, I wish I was more like them."

The tendency to want others to think we have it all together isn't limited to what we buy; it overflows into what we do. We're here, there, and everywhere, filling our calendars with activities and opportunities that mostly benefit ourselves. Spin class on Wednesdays, yoga on Fridays, coffee dates with friends, monthly manicures, cooking class on Monday nights, business networking luncheons, trips to the mall when boredom creeps in. Throw in volunteering at the shelter to "give back." Add a photo of me serving soup to the homeless and post it on Facebook to show the world how balanced I am. Get the kids to soccer, karate, Spanish class, piano, and swimming. Then there's church, where we somehow achieve the "volunteer of the year" badge.

Why do we do this? Somehow we've bought into the idea that cramming in activities that aren't bad for us can provide the purpose we long to find. These activities will make us better. They will make our children well-rounded and keep them out of trouble. Have any of us stopped to notice that all of these activities revolve around us? We've sold ourselves for outward Band-Aids rather than looking at what develops deep, long-lasting results.

Before you know it, you've become a success-crazed, comfort-seeking, status-hungry consumer who thinks she has purpose and deep relationships, but in reality, you lack meaning. You're a rebel without a cause. Do you want to change that? Read on, friend.

Feeling Rebellious?

You must be tired of living like this if you've decided to continue the journey in this book. You won't regret it. I'll never forget when my dissatisfaction started turning into tangible change. I started feeling rebellious, and it felt good. I didn't want any more hamster-wheel, robot living. I knew there was more out there than what the media and magazines were telling me; I just didn't know where to find it. The good news is that I've started to discover where to find it, and I want to share it with you!

However, I should warn you that if you rebel against culture, people aren't going to like it. You'll be questioned, examined, and misunderstood. You'll stick out like a sore thumb. I know this concept freaks some of you right out. I won't lie. All you people-pleaser and peacekeepers will be challenged. Those of you who really struggle with striving for popularity and being liked by everyone will have to abandon that dream. Those who love money and all the comforts it brings will have to be willing to give it up.

Making this change will be a challenge, but I guarantee that it will also be fun! It will inspire those who want something greater but don't know how to get off the moving wheel. Others around you will have a fighting chance at becoming change-agents in their worlds. And most importantly, everything you do will last—even beyond your lifetime. Your life will no longer be void of passion. You will experience the freedom of leaving the ordinary behind you in the dust.

Still here? Good. You are truly ranked among the brave. Let's find out what this rebellion looks like. First, making this change requires several mental switches:

From Success to Surrender

I'll admit it: I love success. I'm an overachiever. Regardless of why I'm an overachiever, the fact remains the same: the value I place on myself is determined by what I achieve. So far, I've tasted a ton of achievement. My ambition has paid off time and time again. But I've found a problem with success. Matthew Barnett calls success "a moving target." I have personally experienced this "poster child" one day, "has-been" the next day. We see this constantly in the life of movie stars. (Does anyone know what happened to Boy George?) Our untelevised lives tell the same story. This fickle attention that society gives us becomes a problem when we strive so hard to get success back after we lose it or when we taste success and fall for the trap of never having enough.

Here's another problem with success: it's all about me. I want the credit, the profile, and the status that comes with it. And even though I really want you to succeed too, if it comes down to whether you or I move ahead, you may just see my inner demon exposed. Yuck, I hate admitting that. I really want you to think differently of me. But who am I kidding? In some dark crevice of my heart lies this truth that I try to ignore.

I've found that the answer to this is in the switch to surrender—surrendering my desire for success. This takes accepting the truth that if I accomplish nothing in this life, I'm enough. For an overachiever, this was a very hard pill for me to swallow.

I've been trying this switch out, and I can tell you that it's been freeing. I've been daily surrendering my idea of making others think I'm a success. Sometimes that's what we want more than success itself: the "appearance" of success. Today, I'm more willing to show my weaknesses. I've stopped striving. I've given up the notion that everyone will love me and want me on their team. I'm renewing my mind so that I don't even think along the lines of how successful I'm being but instead focus on how much I'm surrendering.

Surrender isn't a popular concept in the mind of the self-absorbed, but it goes further (like surrender isn't painful enough). It gets worse. It moves from surrender to my own success to wanting others to succeed. I've done this a couple of times, and both felt awful. I've actually given up positions for myself in order to promote others. Big cheer for Connie? That's not why I'm sharing this. I share this because I don't want you to think that this is some "good-karma" strategy that will promote you to limits beyond your wildest dreams. No, some people won't even thank you. They'll even forget you. They may even stab you in the back. But the reactions of society don't matter anymore; what matters is that there's a real transformation that is happening in you. I know what you're thinking, "This is *good*?" Yes, because you've just surrendered your god of success. If you can move on, its power on you is loosened, and now you're finally free to make some real impact on yourself and the world around you. It's warped, I know. Read on, brave one.

The Switch from Material Poverty to Spiritual Riches

Everything you give away, you get to keep. If you don't get it, don't worry, because you will. "Material *poverty*?" Did you think I meant to say "wealth??" That's the interesting thing about excessive material wealth; it brings a poverty of the soul. "The most common view of Americans of poverty is the absence of things," Richard Stearns has said. In all our abundance, we live in a nation of enormous poverty of spirit.

Let's start with the problem: money, or more specifically, our love of it. It's not really the money itself that we love, but what it brings, namely freedom and independence. I feel a little Beyonce coming on as I charge it again: "All the women who are independent, throw your hands up at me." I'm throwing my hands up! They're waving in the air as the store clerk rings in my latest purchase, proving I'm every woman! More Beyonce! "Girl, I didn't know you could get down like that—"

Yet, in his book *Rediscovering Values*, Jim Wallis discusses how most people who are wealthy almost *never* feel secure in their wealth. Apparently, those with a net worth of half a million to a million felt they could survive better on two million. You and I think that's a little loopy, don't we? I'm no different. Whatever my net worth was like last year, I think I'd be better off with at *least* ten thousand added on. Wait, maybe twenty. Okay, fifty.

Studies show the growing gap between the rich and the poor. Economic booms only enhance the greed of those who have plenty and keep the poor on a hamster wheel of poverty. The middle class, trying to keep up, dig themselves further into piles of debt trying to keep up by buying more houses, cars, clothes, and "toys" they don't need. In the city where I live, the cost of an average, middle-class individual has increased 134 percent since the 1980s. In 2008, child poverty rose from fifty-three thousand to seventy-three thousand in one year. Many of these children have both parents working full-time, which shows that having a job is no longer a way out of poverty. The city where I live has a large homeless population that goes to work but calls a shelter home. This includes homeless families that travel from church basement to church basement each night.

It is this exact knowledge that has completely messed up my life as of late. It has impacted me so much that I thought I'd mess up your life with it too. (You can thank me later). But as you can guess, it gets worse, but only from a certain perspective.

I've done some research on the world economy, and I'm discovering that my measly income of forty thousand a year really *is* wealthy. The massive gap between the rich and the poor extends around the globe. It is completely unjust. Before you think I'm going to tell you about starving children in Africa and make you feel guilty, let me disarm you by saying I'm not going to do that. I'm actually going to go deeper.

Did you know that the top 20 percent of the world (that's us) consumes 86 percent of the world's (not ours) goods (Richard Stearns, *Hole in our Gospel*)? That tells me something about our nation: we're a greedy bunch. We don't do what we continuously nag our kids to do—share. We hold on to our money like there isn't enough for all. We don't practice what we preach. And the scary truth is that I'm a part of it.

Before you think of me as a Bono-type advocate, hear me out. I've lived in ignorance about what my greed was doing to people; these were the people who live outside of "me" and "my own little world." One plus one is two. Two plus two is four. Four plus four is eight. Eight plus eight is sixteen. Sixteen plus sixteen is—well, you get the point. I don't write this to show you my math skills. I actually had to stop at sixteen because I couldn't figure it out without a calculator. I write this to remind us about the truth and power of multiplication. One little, two little, three little consumers added onto four little, five little, six selfish spenders make for a multitude of hoarders oblivious to a world in need around them. And before I excuse myself from the equation, it can all be traced back to me sitting in the corner, clutching and stroking my money.

Forgive me, but I didn't know that our world produces enough resources for all its inhabitants to eat and survive. I was oblivious, and I thought people were suffering because of their laziness or lack of luck in their birthplace. But the truth remains that the "poor are hungry, and their hunger keeps them poor" (Richard Stearns).

Poverty is society's problem. You and I steward answers and solutions to these problems of poverty. We just can't see them because we're stuck in a matrix called "the mall." Under its spell, we remain unable to see the needs of the world.

If you're feeling rebellious, I dare you to stop clutching your money and live with an open hand. As quickly as it comes to you, after you take care of your living expenses, then give the rest away. A bit crazy? Perhaps. There's a whole movement of people in our world who are downsizing from their oversized homes and who are taking care of their basic living expenses only to give the rest of their incomes away. This may repulse you, but to me, it sounds rather exciting. However, in order to ever think of trying something as crazy as this, we need to become more disciplined in how we spend and save.

I mentioned that everything you give away, you get to keep. If you can stomach more, I'll explain that soon (if you haven't figured it out already). But before you read another word, I dare you to do something. I dare you to take twenty dollars out of your pocket right now and give it away. First, it will open your eyes to see someone who needs it. You may have passed them time and time again but never truly saw their need. When your eyes actively look for someone in need, you'll be amazed at how much you've been missing! Why do this? The purpose of this is to bless someone else, someone who is not you. It may mean giving up five Starbucks visits, but is that really so bad? Time to find the coffeemaker at home that has been buried under the deep fryer, waffle iron, and juicer since your wedding— I hope this challenge starts to show you that money is really just money and that through the act of giving it away, I hope the mighty dollar begins to lose its luster in your heart.

From Comfort to Security

This is the fun section! Who doesn't want to be comfortable? I love my sweatpants. When I come home after a day of "bling" and tight jeans, I'm itching to get into my sweats and Run-D.M.C. T-shirt. No wonder I love teaching hip-hop; I have the most comfortable work attire in the world! When I'm not dancing in my sweats, I'm sitting in them and reading. Actually, I should say *trying* to read between my five-year-old telling me the same butt joke for the twentieth time and my one-year-old who has gone from unraveling all the toilet paper to eating the dog food.

You know what's the hardest thing about my sweats? Taking them off. There are some days I find myself strategizing how I can justify wearing them out to my next networking meeting. Maybe a nice scarf will dress them up? No, my fate is clear: the sweats must come off. My attachment to my sweats reminds me of the problem with comfort: the more comfortable we are, the more we want to stay in that place.

Ever found yourself on a super comfy couch in a furniture store where they have conveniently put their largest flat-screen right there in front of it? Ah, yes— You could stay there all day. Just head over in your pajamas or in my case, my sweats, and have a day away. Who needs the spa! This is much more cost-effective. Why not invite a friend too, and make sure to fill a bag with your own drinks and popcorn! If you're lucky, they've put on a good movie and placed one of those electrical fireplaces right next to you. Everything is set up to be a perfect girl's day out—that is, until the furniture store kicks you out. Good-bye cost-effective, comfy couch—

We are obsessed with our own comfort. I'm not just talking about furniture and clothing; I'm talking about where we place ourselves socially and economically. Pretty much everything I buy is for my own comfort. My circle of friends makes me comfortable. When I lose my friends or the stuff I've bought, I lose not only all sense of comfort but my security as well. And security is a feeling that everyone deserves.

Try this to test your comfort level: The next time you see a homeless person, go up and talk to him or her. Introduce yourself. Engage in conversation. Feeling uncomfortable? Or find the oddest, weirdest, smelliest person in the lunchroom at work and sit with them. Sure, it may turn out to be your boss, but you can tolerate him or her for an hour, right? This kind of challenge may almost send the introverts into cardiac arrest. I'm sure even the extroverts shuddered.

I remember the first time I decided to approach a homeless man. I was scared of his tattered clothes and toothless smile. I mustered up the courage to ask him what he needed. He began to tell me how he was living with his sister and was looking for bottles to help with groceries. I gave him some bottles I had in my van and drove off, wondering why I had been so afraid of these people. Turns out being toothless doesn't mean you're an ax murderer. My five-year-old and I now carry care packages in our van with water, a bus ticket, gloves in the winter, and some granola bars. We take the time to talk to the homeless when we meet them on the street and find out their names. One time, a homeless man was so touched with the care package my son gave him that he went dumpster-diving for a gift for my son and brought out a *bong*. My son, having no clue what it was, thought it was the coolest thing he'd ever seen! I, on the other hand, thanked the man graciously for the gift while I tried to plan how I'd explain my son walking down the street with such an item. (For those wondering, we didn't keep the bong.)

I think it's good for us to do something that makes us completely uncomfortable every once and awhile. It's a good raise in the humility-o-meter, and it reminds us not to take ourselves so seriously. If you would like more tangible ideas, you can find out all the crazy things me and others do to keep uncomfortable on my blog at culturerebel.com.

If you stay within the walls of your comfort zone, you're missing out on a world of new opportunities that you could be experiencing. Like how I got into hip-hop dance. There I was—a very overweight twenty-two-year-old standing in a hip-hop class full of teensy-weensy, sexy people. It didn't help that hip-hop is a bouncy dance; when I danced, everything on my overweight body bounced. *Everything!* It was intimidating, but I loved dancing hip-hop too much to let my fears get the better of me. Sixteen years later, not only has it kept me fit, but it is now my main profession. If I hadn't allowed myself to suffer discomfort back then, I wouldn't have the opportunities that I do now, specifically teaching in schools and producing shows about social justice issues.

"Preoccupation with safety can get in the way of living full lives. We begin thinking of what we want to prevent and avoid rather than what we want to encourage and develop," Alan Hirsch once said. Ironically, the more uncomfortable we allow ourselves to be, the more we can discover true security. We're so afraid to fail; however, I've learned the best nuggets in life through failure and allowing myself to look a little silly. Peter Druckner stated once that those who take risks make about two big mistakes a year. Those who don't take risks? Well, they made about two big mistakes a year too! Interesting.

So, get out there and do something that scares the snot out of you! Do something wild and crazy! Show yourself you're not so fixated on your own comfortable world! There's something for you to discover! And if any repercussions arise from my advice, you did *not* hear any of it from me (because I didn't mean *that*)! Lastly, have fun!

From Desperate to Dangerous

You are not called to be hot. It is not meant to be your life's ambition. If it's not our main purpose, then why does it seem every media medium is trying to tell us that this should be our top priority? If I'm not called to be hot, then what on earth am I called to?

Ever think, "I used to be pretty," or "I wish I was beautiful?" I'm finding that a lot of women echo the same statement. Just the other week, I was looking through photos of me in my late twenties. I couldn't help but think, "Wow! I was so ... thin!" I can't believe that back then I thought I was chubby. I started scrutinizing myself then compared to now. Well, that's not fair. Back then, I was kidless and in my twenties! We're talking before gray hairs and the aftermath of baby flubber. Now I know it's time to hit the hair salon when my bunch—not just a few, a *bunch*—of gray hairs show up. (They've migrated to my eyebrows too. Who gets gray in their *eyebrows?*) Now, instead of looking for my skinny's, I'm looking for my spanks.

Many mourn the weight they were back in their teens. There's where I can find some comfort. I was heavy as a teen. I actually weigh less now after my second baby, so I can't empathize with those gals. But I understand mourning past weight from before baby. I have all these awesome clothes that I can't fit into. For now, I'm stuck with two outfits that actually fit. And God forbid … the other day I checked myself in a three-way mirror. *Is my butt really that big? And for heaven's sake, why did someone not tell me I have a double chin?*

I remember in grade five, I decided to ask to be beautiful for Christmas. That's all I wanted. I didn't ask Santa for that one. Nope, I went to the Big Guy and asked Him to take my chubs away, fix my teeth, and make me breathtakingly beautiful. I woke up Christmas morning, avoiding the mirror right away as I wanted to be sure to give God thanks for the amazing gift of beauty He had given me that morning. After I poured out my heart of thanks, I approached the mirror with great expectation only to find my buck teeth and chubby stature still reflected in front of me. I was devastated.

Years would go by of bullying, boys mocking me by saying; "I don't know why you're going to the dance. No one would dance with you because you're so ugly." Alas, I was quite the ugly duckling. I still cringe at pictures a bit. I would find comfort when some well-intentioned adult would say, "Don't worry. It's just baby fat. You'll grow out of it." When the "baby fat" was still there in grade twelve, I wondered when this would ever happen. And note that no one ever said I'd "grow out" of my teeth. Perhaps they knew that was a lost cause—

I turned out to be an average-looking teen. A definite step up from childhood post-braces, but still Connie Chunk nonetheless. A mentor in my life said to me during my teen years, "You and I are just average-looking people." She then pointed out a couple of girls we both knew who were as she stated, "really beautiful." At the time, my heart was crushed. You mean I was *average*? I wanted to beautiful like the other girls!

I *am* average. You're not going to see me on the cover of a magazine, not even on days I put in a lot of effort. I'm at peace with "average." My husband doesn't seem to mind "average." The only thing I don't want to be is "cute." Try calling me that and see what happens. Unfortunately, my hubby says that's exactly what I am—cute. Urgh.

It's that exact word that makes me spend so much money. I'm trying hard to ditch the "cute" and get the "hot." A new outfit, highlights, a little tan, maybe a bit more blingy earrings, and as uncomfortable they are (and even *more* uncomfortable when carrying children), I'll force myself into heels if that means "cute" has left the building. What's wrong with cute? Marketing doesn't sell cute. It sells sexy. It sells "hot." "Cute" just isn't good enough.

"Though we long to be found attractive, we were made to notice others" (Margot Starbuck, *Unsqueezed*). Brilliant. I want to do that, but it's harder than I thought. It's hard to let go of the self-obsessing. It's embarrassing when my husband is the one catching me in the act of "checking out" other women. It takes discipline to walk into a room and not think about what I'm wearing or if the wind completely wrecked the hour I just spent on my hair and focus on others in the room who deserve my undivided attention.

It's hard to live in a world where Eva Longoria is the standard for middle-aged women. We have to stop being mentored by *The Real Housewives*. Whether we care to admit it, *Desperate Housewives* has sold us a message we're buying into. Without realizing it, we have sold out for a life of self-objectification. We buy into the media's lie that we are an object to be viewed, so you'd better give them a view worth looking at. If you're a really good view, marketers will post you up on billboards to help them sell billions of dollars' worth of products. Your picture will inspire young girls and women to do all they can to become just like you. You will model for men the way a woman was created to be viewed and treated. You will cause mass eating disorders.

The problem with self-objectification is that it oppresses women. It silences their voices. It shuts down desire to rise to leadership roles that don't involve a modeling contract. It blinds our eyes to the answer we can be to social justice issues in our communities. It dumbs a woman down to the point she won't aspire to anything but a posing object. Deep inside her could be the heart of an Olympic athlete, a CEO, or a philanthropist, but it would never be known because of the tormented mindset she's been sold.

Just before you have excused yourself from thinking you are a victim of self-objectification, see if one or more of these apply to you.

- The number on the scale determines your mood for the day.
- You keep track of how many people comment or "like" your new profile pic.
- You are keenly aware of how many men have looked at you while you were walking down the mall. (You think this is only for the single women? Married women do this too.)
- If men aren't looking at you today, you feel you need to "step up your game" by getting your hair fixed, going for a tan, and putting on more makeup. (Again, married women are not excluded from this circus.)
- You would never dream of leaving the house without makeup.
- You hate not feeling sexy.
- You struggle with your eating; either not eating or eating too much.
- You crave praise from your fellow females and love feeling like the "alpha."
- You have a hard time not thinking about your body all the time.
- You obsess about what goes in your mouth.
- You compare yourself with other women.
- When a woman steps up to speak, you're thinking more about what she's wearing than what she's saying.
- You read fashion magazines for inspiration.

As a result, we have a pandemic of women who are losing desire for their husbands and engaging in casual flirting (that sometimes spiral places they didn't intend). All in the name of just wanting someone to validate their outward appearance. The problem goes further. While we obsess, our daughters are watching and following in our footsteps. Young women are following our example, causing a movement of girls starting as young as age eight thinking their only reason for existence is to look like a supermodel. We have failed them, ladies. We have distracted them from their real purpose by our own stupidity. Our boob jobs and tummy tucks tell them they are not beautiful the way they are. Our self-hatred speech is teaching them how to talk and think about themselves. While we've been obsessing about ourselves in the mirror, the young girls of our nation have grown up way too fast, allowing boys to treat them like the objects we've allowed them to believe they are. We owe them an apology. It's time we start being the role models they deserve.

The good news is that you don't have to fall for this any longer. You can be free from self-obsessing to become who you were created for. You weren't created to be desperate. You were created to be *dangerous*. You have life-changing impact living inside of you. *That's* what is going to make you beautiful and vibrant, not another Botox treatment. Dangerous will look good on you. Go try that on for size.

From Status to Love

I'm still in Starbucks. You may have had a lot of things happen in your life up to this point. Perhaps your days turned into weeks, and your weeks turned into months. You may have a new hairstyle (looks great, by the way). You may now have a child, and you may have seen that same child graduate. (Wow, it's been awhile!) But for me, I have not moved. I have been typing my heart out while drinking my coffee and looking up occasionally at my surroundings, all while suffering from a severe case of "numb bum."

Right now, there's a group of teen girls talking giddily at the table across from me. A married couple is locked in intense conversation to the left. Yikes, that doesn't look good. Let's move on—a father and daughter on a coffee date (*awww!*) and some Rabbi-looking guy who is also typing on a computer. (Maybe he's writing an exegete of the Koran.) I digress.

These very quick glances remind me of how relationships really are the essence of the human race. That's why businesses like Starbucks survive and thrive, because they're places where people can connect (and where moms can also gain a slight bit of sanity by hitting the drive-throughs).

A whole book could be written on relationships and all its issues. Come to think of it, I believe a "couple" of books have been written on the subject. That's what I gathered while I was walking through the massive self-help and psychology sections in Chapters. We're focusing on switching gears. We want to move from being someone who just follows pop culture and believes everything it tells us to becoming rebellious of it. In terms of relationships, that's the switch from one who is focused on status to one who is rooted in love.

Ever watch the movie *Mean Girls* with Lindsay Lohan? It's my guilty pleasure. Takes me right back to high school. The sad thing is that I see the same thing in my adult world; it just looks more diplomatic and dignified. Just when you think the "Regina George's" of the world will remain in the halls of your senior high school, think again. They're in your playgroups, school council committees, and church. They may even live next door. A couple of them are your Facebook friends. You may just be one of them.

"Status anxiety" is a term employed by Alain de Bottom. He states that status anxiety occurs when we are attempting to climb the social ladder. The anxiety part happens when we become obsessed with how we are perceived by others. The result? Comparison frenzy! Benjamin Franklin once said, "To find out a girl's faults, praise her to her girlfriends." "Envy is a symptom of a lack of appreciation of our own uniqueness and self-worth" (Elizabeth O'Connor).

The problem gets exposed when we base who we are on what others think of us. Label someone a slut, and he or she may just act like one. Label someone a snob, and he or she becomes one. Why? Because we start perceiving ourselves the way others see us. State something long enough, and you'll own it. It's a strange phenomenon. I can't help but wonder what would have happened if we had labeled each person differently.

It all stems from our deep longing to be loved and accepted. We want to be in the "right social circle." You know, the ones who look like they're having so much fun, the ones who post the most amazing pictures of the parties they throw on their Facebook walls (the parties they forgot to invite you to).

I hate the idea of groups. Who created that absurd concept? People are so beautiful in all forms. One of my favorite quotes is this: "The problem of standards of beauty is they create standards of ugliness" (Alan Hirsch). I learn much from those who speak and look differently than me. But again, to experience this takes us back to chapter four. Seth Godin tells us why there are groups in his book *We're All Weird*. (You've got to buy the book just to look at the front cover!). He states, "If I can tell you that some other group is wrong, not just different, but wrong, then I increase my power over you. Us and not us is a dead end." When I read that, I stopped dead in my tracks. I'm a defender of the underdog and have no problems fighting against the injustice of elitism. However, when I read this, I realized that I was contributing to the two different groups, the "us" and "not us" groups.

It's one thing to have power over people because people fear you; it's another thing to have power over people because you're fighting for them. Both are equally wrong. This is a sobering thought for us underdog fighters. We already know how shallow those who lord their rule over the weak are. It sickens us to see people suck up to them to gain approval and popularity. But have we ever thought how wrong it is for us to gain power in the name of "fighting for equality?" My heart's just as wretched when I get an inner sense of joy when I gain another loyal follower who also begins to detest those who reign in the realm of the elite. Just a thought—

People are crying for genuine relationships. We are worlds apart from one another because we have created an alternate world of relationships based on where you can get me on the ladder of status, how perfect I can present myself, and what power and influence I can carry over others. The more influential I am, the more people want to know me. The more people want to know me, the more power I have. The more power I have, the better I feel about myself … until my alternative world crashes down and I get hurt. Any life built on anything less than vulnerability will always have to fight to stay where it is on the cultural status hierarchy. That's the problem with food chains; someone always gets eaten. And we wonder why mass fortresses of protection guard our hearts.

I watched the most fascinating *TED Talks* video featuring Brene Brown, who has spent years studying those who live lives that are open and vulnerable. Being vulnerable isn't easy. I think it would be easier to stand outside naked for a moment of mocking than to unveil the inner-self to others for a lifetime of judgment. Brown states that in order for us to connect, we have to allow ourselves to be *seen*. This is scary for the shy and the outspoken because we all think the same thing: *Is there something about me that if people knew, they would withdraw from me?*

Every soul cries, "Am I worthy of connection?" We then allow the mass public to tell us the answer. Please note that unstable analysis can never end well, no matter how popular one may seem. This leads us to live in shame of who we are. Brown describes shame as "the fear of connection." We live in a world of people full of shame. We're scared to death of each other!

What would it look like to be free of this shame? What differentiates the open and vulnerable from the ones cowering in the corner? "Those who feel worthy have a strong sense of love and belonging and *believe* they're worthy of it" (Brene Brown). That may just be the most courageous act you and I ever engage ourselves in—the belief that we are worthy to give love and receive love.

Friends, we can either think being vulnerable will lead to a life of shame or see it as the beginning of the life we were created for, a life of joy, creativity, belonging, and love. Imagine for a moment what that life could look like: a life free of having to prove yourself to others. A life free of questioning your every word and movement. A life free of checking yourself out in the mirror every moment in fear your hair may have moved out of place. Those who have discovered this kind of life become *safe* people, people who provide love, safety, and comfort for weary souls around them. Sounds like the One I've given my life to follow. I believe with all my heart *this* is the kind of life we were made for.

The switch one must make to become a culture rebel in the realm of relationships means that one must go from being status-driven to knowing he or she are worth loving. If you and I know this truth in the depths of our souls, then we can freely extend love—even to an enemy. We can live with open arms, and we can extend them even to the shallowest of people. I was deeply challenged by this concept while I was reading the book *Nurture* by Lisa Bevere. In her book, she writes the following:

> The need for connection is more viable than the need for food. And as women, we have the ability to connect people. We have lost the ability to understand the importance of connection. People need to know that they are watched for. People need to know that they are welcomed. They need to know they are safe and that somebody is going to have what they need to make it. Far too many women are disconnected and isolated. Others want desperately to connect but don't know how to see this happen. We are heartsick and in need of intimate, safe connections so we can in turn heal and help others. Are we far too busy surviving to make the time to assure that the tender lives surrounding us thrive? We are far too guarded, wounded, and afraid to open our lives to the possibility of connections from an "imperfect" other ... When you are isolated, your world revolves around you, your problems and your own perspective. This fosters excessive self-consciousness. We imagine everyone is looking at us and talking about us, because we are all we think about. The only cure for this is to realize the world is way bigger than we know.

Use your life to truly embrace and welcome others in so they can flourish. Sounds more exciting than being popular, doesn't it? Sounds like culture rebel kind of living.

All of this will cost you. I've spent so much time with you now that I can't just let you believe that this "higher road" will lead to the rose garden. Saint Augustine was right when he stated, "Every new love contains the seeds of fresh sorrows." People will be mean. You'll think they couldn't go lower, and then they will. They will hurt you, and you will look weak. You will lose your place on the status food chain. Are you okay with all of this? Can you let go of a false world of connection and embrace one that is real? Can you believe you are worthy of love when you receive none? Once your broken heart and the root of love meet, that's when you're ready to discover how worthy of love you really are.

C. S. Lewis once said the following:

> Love anything, and your heart will certainly be wrung and possibly be broken. If you want to make sure of keeping it intact, you must give your heart to no one, not even to an animal. Wrap it carefully round with hobbies and little luxuries; avoid all entanglements; lock it up safe in the casket or coffin of your selfishness. But in that casket—safe, dark, motionless, airless—it will change. It will not be broken; instead it will become unbreakable, impenetrable, irredeemable.

Choosing the road of loving others regardless and knowing you are worthy of love will revolutionize your relationships.

From Consumer to Steward

My husband calls me the perfect consumer. He's right. I'll see the latest item on an ad, and I'm sold! He watches my eyes glimmer as the commercial carries on about how their latest technology can solve all my acne problems. The transformation I see on the screen is unbelievable. I'm off to the Internet to order myself some of this amazing product, and I don't even have acne!

When I met my husband, I was impressed with how he saved money. Now I find it simply annoying. I didn't realize marrying him meant he'd want me to save too! I have a nickname for him. I call him "Big Brother" because when I go out, he is watching (insert scary music here). Somehow, he knows where I was and what I bought.

All jokes aside, I know my husband is right. I have spent much of my life consuming rather than producing. Even as a child, I would spend my allowance on candy the moment it was given to me. You could say I have a problem: I'm a shop-a-holic. But before I continue to paint consumerism in a terrible light, let's make a culture rebel switch! We all have to buy things (and it's okay to have nice things too), so let's change our focus from being consumed to being a steward.

When I give my son money, I see how well he is at following in my footsteps. He has visions of the toy store in his mind. What's cute is that he thinks five cents makes him rich and able to buy anything his heart desires. What I would love my son to do is to honor the gift I've given him, the gift of independence and freedom from mommy for a brief moment. I want him to think about what he will do with it, not just spend it on the first candy he sees. I see a bigger picture. I see that in a moment, candy will be gone and that he will have nothing—no more candy and no more money. In that moment, I will ask him, "Now, son, was that brief moment worth your money?"

He will look up at me with his sweet blue eyes and say, "*Yes!* Can I have another dime?"

Oh boy—

We are all consumers. "Consumer" means one who consumes. Profound, I know. The question is this: *What* are we consuming? Are we consumers of the good, or are we consumers of the artificial? If you want to know where your heart is, just take a look at your Visa bill. Dick Staub says, "They encourage us to shop, convincing us that shopping will do today what it failed to do yesterday." Who are "they?" "They" are the mass marketers who are making culture. They are forming our minds, whether we want to conform to their thinking or not. What they want to do is reach into our insecurities and pull out a material solution to our deepest longings.

That reminds me of the time I went to get my eyebrows waxed. I was pregnant with our second son and feeling that lovely "preggo-frump." As I lay in the chair (as relaxed as you can be when someone is ripping hair out from your face), the consultant said to me, "You know, you have blotchy skin." That's it. That's all she said. That's all she had to say. Immediately, my mind started racing: "Oh, those pregnancy hormones, they're messing up my face! I can't believe I've been showing my blotchy face in public!"

After a few minutes, she gently offered the answer to my very new skin problem: "We have a wonderful product that will clear that right up for you." Oh, the relief. She had an answer to my problem. Actually, she had an answer for my insecurity—that is, the brand new insecurity that she had revealed. I look back and realize what a brilliant salesperson she was! If I were a business owner, she'd be my girl. What was meant to be only a ten-dollar sale turned out to be a two-*hundred*-dollar sale. She was thrilled! I was cured! My husband was ticked.

When you and I go to the mall, we're not looking for basic human needs. No, we're looking for an experience. We're looking for something that promises us that our outward appearance will be transformed, thus revolutionizing our social life. We want a "look" that will define us, something we can cling to for meaning. It's not just a bra; it has turned me into a sex kitten. It's not just a straightener; it's given me a whole new outlook on life. It's not just a shirt; it's given me a new start after a bad relationship. That lipstick states that I'm fierce; I look just like Halle Berry. We will be complete when our kitchen has been renovated; I'll finally be free to invite people over without embarrassment.

What are we doing? We're finding purpose and meaning in superficial things that we will only need more of to get that feeling back. How is this any different than a junkie looking for the next fix? The consumer is promised more than just the experience. "You can have all this *now*. You don't have to wait! No money? No problem!" They've got a payment plan that will work for you, and if they don't, you've got plenty of credit … on the "other" card that hasn't been racked up yet. The promise is there, but it can't deliver; it can't give you purpose. And although you can have it now, it will cost you a ton of stress and financial burden on your family. Is that your purpose?

I know you don't want to hear this because it's hard to hear. I don't even want to hear it, but we need to. These daily messages to buy and invest in ourselves are everywhere. Look for them. You'll start to see them at every turn! You'll be surprised by how much you're being preached at throughout your day without even knowing it. This is how culture is made. Groups of people have decided to make their voices the loudest. In the book *The Tipping Point*, Malcolm Gladwell tells the story of how it only takes 150 people to change the world. We need to stop allowing ourselves to become passive, apathetic, robotic people who don't see life outside purchasing the latest flat-screen and upgrading our cars. Where's that getting us? Absolutely nowhere, but man, our houses look great. And our kids have got the best of the best. They've got the newest Apple inventions. My baby's got the top-of-the-line ExerSaucer. I may not have any money saved up for their postsecondary education, but man, they're living the life! Meanwhile, many of these suburban rich kids become addicted to greed, sending them out to spend money in places like the drug world or strip clubs. Oh, you didn't know that? We've taught them consumerism, to want more of everything, and so more they will seek. We've created a family culture that loves to look good and have the right stuff while inside our four walls we are falling apart. All this "stuff" is killing our hearts. This is the "good life?"

The answer is to become a steward rather than a self-consumed consumer. If I gave you something precious to me to hold onto, I know you would do your best to take good care of it. Yes, you may break it or lose it, but I know you would have tried your best to keep it intact for me. We're built that way. We're built to take good care of things. Instead of thinking that your money and your stuff is yours to splurge on for your own gain, why not see yourself as a steward who's been entrusted with all this stuff?

Why not think of the job you have as a gift that's been given to you to take care of yourself and your family and as something that can be a great investment? I don't know about you, but when it comes to investing, I'm careful where I put my money. I don't want to just put it anywhere. I give it careful thought. When I started to think of all my stuff, my money, and my work in that light, it changed my entire pattern of thinking. Now, instead of spending money on useless things, I think about where it's going. Will I invest it in things like the candy my son loves to buy, which is gone in a second and which leaves me nothing? Or can I invest my money somewhere that will give a great return one day? To be a culture rebel, you need to let go of the temporal and give more thought to what lasts.

Take a look at your Visa bill. Do you see anything repeated continually? Lunches out? Clothes? Big-ticket items? What is this saying about you? Who knew your Visa bill could serve as a heart monitor?! Are these items serving your insecurities, greed, and inner desires? Have they fulfilled that for you, or have they left you only wanting more? What's the real underlining motivation for buying them? Dig deep. Now, instead of getting all down on yourself, make a plan for how you can better steward what's been given to you. What can you live without? You'd be surprised at how much you can comfortably let go of! Don't do it all at once. Tackle one item at a time. Maybe it starts with cutting seven coffees a week down to three. Maybe it's avoiding the mall for one month just to see if you can do it. Maybe you could invite someone over for lunch rather than going out. Whatever it is, know that your switch from consumer to steward will have its bumps, but it's worth the ride. My journey has opened my eyes to see how tightly I was holding onto my stuff.

For example, I recently cleaned out my closet. I found *eleven* lululemon tanks. *Eleven.* I don't work out enough to justify that. I also found *seven* adidas jackets—six of them which I recently gave away to audience members at a hip-hop show I produced on poverty issues. I am now on a journey to not buy any new clothing for one year. It may kill me, but I *want* to do it. I want to prove to myself that I really don't need half of what I buy, especially when it comes to clothes. How many clothing items have I bought just for the sake of the almighty "sale?" It was only ten dollars, yet I have four similar items already. "Sale" has messed with my mind one too many times. I have found better options in clothing swaps, secondhand stores, and consignment shops.

People are catching this new concept of stewardship. One of the malls in the city I live in has a program called "Role Mothers." Because most of their shopping population consists of moms, they decided to take on this idea of encouraging women to be good stewards of their money and to know the balance between having nice things and giving back to the community. Role Mothers connects moms with organizations in the city where they can volunteer with their families. What an innovative concept for a mall! You can find out more about what they do in my list of culture rebels in the back of the book.

Friends, live free of selfish consumption. When we finally let go, we are free to be the producers we were called to be. You were not created to consume only, but also to produce.

From Isolation to Community

One of my favorite shows of the nineties is *Seinfeld*. I loved watching how Jerry, Elaine, George, and Kramer's lives wove together through their endless "normality" of relationship issues, mishaps, and mundane days. It gave me warm, fuzzy feelings of camaraderie. I'd turn off the TV, feeling like I had just been invited into their lives.

One of the hardest things I've experienced in my thirties is loneliness. When I was single and even into the early years of being newly married, I was always surrounded by amazing friends. Weekends were full of exciting adventures or just lounging together at someone's house. It was truly an electric time. There's nothing like having a safe group of friends who accept and love you. We could have taken on the world.

I'm not sure when that changed. It could have been when we moved to a new city and I found myself at home with a newborn. It was hard to start from rock bottom, trying to find good friend material, and then to begin the hard work of building each relationship.

I had never been hurt by shallow people until my thirties. For the longest time, I wondered if they truly existed outside junior high, but they do. Wondering who I could trust, I responded to the hurt by isolating myself from the world. I started building a sense of community on Facebook, where I could put my best face forward. Yet Facebook sank me into more loneliness and depression than I could ever imagine. On Facebook, people would "friend" me only to ignore me in public. On my birthday, over two thousand "happy birthdays" would hit my wall, but I was still lonely and dying for someone to go for coffee with. If I found someone I was finally beginning to connect with, I would soon see all the parties they threw that I was not invited to. I started to see my "friends" interacting with one another on their walls but not on mine. They would "like" one another's statuses, leaving mine void of any "likes" from them.

I started to become very self-conscious and guarded. I suddenly felt this grade eight feeling well up in my body. I decided to commit to *not* "liking" their statuses! "Take *that*." If I had a party, I'd be sure to post pictures of all the fun we had without any of them. I'd put comments on the pictures like "Best party ever with the best people." (How old am I?) I started carrying my camera everywhere, taking pictures with all my friends just to be able to post my amazing life for the world to see. "And here we are at the homeless shelter—" Gag me. I was making myself sick.

I didn't like who I was becoming. I was morphing into a shallow soul who only saw people as photo ops for my Facebook charade. I didn't like who I had become, but I didn't know how to live any other way. I wasn't finding deep friendships, so I had to create a world where it at least looked like I had them. The result? My loneliness was turning into some serious depression.

I remember the day I chose a new focus for my Facebook page. My goal was to stop treating it as my social empire but as an opportunity to encourage and network with some amazing people. I would limit my time on it and pick up the phone. I committed to investing in people. I started watching for girls I call "kindred spirits" and dared to ask them to be my friends. Surprisingly, I found some who agreed. I stopped trying to be the most popular person and engaged in a meaningful community with a handful of people. It has been refreshing.

I learned another valuable lesson through my Facebook journey: when haters try to destroy my spirit, I need to let it go. This has been hard to do at times, but the exercise of letting go is always freeing. I've learned that for every hater, there are always a dozen people who love my heart. Why focus on the ones who don't care to understand? I moved on and chose not to open my mouth to speak against them. Seth Godin states, "It is human nature to be weird, but also human nature to be lonely. This conflict between fitting in and standing out is at the core of who we are."

Community is a hard thing to find, but I can guarantee you that it's not found when you try to put your semi-fake best face forward online. It's not found on Twitter where you network with some amazing people, but they're not your kindreds. It's not built on texts sent from your cell phone. It comes from a willingness to be vulnerable. It takes phone calls, coffees dates, and finding the right people to build your life with. Sometimes the long, hard path is just finding the right people—people you really love and feel you can give to and receive from, people who you won't take for granted and who won't use you, people who show up when tragedy strikes and who let you in when they need support, people whom you stick with (and who stick with you) through disagreements and misunderstandings, people you would have over to your home, even when it looks like a bomb went off, and people who don't scream when you show up in jogging pants and no makeup. (Now *that's* friendship.)

Community is messy. It forces us to let go of our perfect images and embrace the mess. It takes courage to allow yourself to be fully immersed in that kind of chaos. You need to be willing to love people without wanting anything in return. You have to let go of building relationships just for the benefit of where they will get you. True friendship and love is built on sacrifice and generosity that is completely selfless.

Perhaps you feel let down by relationships in your life? The only relationships you have in your life now are those that you allow. If you're being used and abused, however, you're the only one who can get out of that. Sometimes we have to say, "Thanks, but no thanks," and have enough self-respect to walk away. It's not wrong to walk away from relationships that are damaging. Some of you need to reread that sentence.

Perhaps you've been so driven by climbing the social ladder that you've actually fooled yourself into thinking you care about the people who surround you. You may care about the ones who have got you where you are, but who have you stepped on to get there? You may not want to dig up those repressed memories because then you may have to admit that you've been pretty shallow and that would be hard. I've been in this place, and it's incredibly humbling; however, it will free you to be the loving person you truly are. Sometimes we have to let go of what we know in order to embrace something better.

Community isn't instant. It takes time to find and then even more time to build. You'll be tempted to give up and head back to your isolated tavern behind a screen, but don't do it. Take the harder road. Show who you truly are and love every ounce of yourself and others. Love when you've been hurt. Forgive those who've hurt you and move forward. See value in people who are completely different than you. You weren't called to live life alone but in genuine friendships.

Culture Rebels Wanted

The world needs people who are brave enough to rebel. Are you one of these? Are you curious about what it feels like to live your full life as a culture rebel? Not just read about it but truly live it? There's a world that needs you and what you offer. There's something very special about your life and what you have in your hands. I know nothing is in your hand right now—except this book and that trail mix you're juggling. I'm talking about the gift inside you—what you do that's unique and special. You hold an answer to a problem that's out there, and it's waiting for you to solve it.

The only way to be different is to live differently, to embrace a life that looks like what we've discussed thus far. Susan B. Anthony, a civil rights activist and pioneer of the women's suffrage movement in the United States, said, "Cautious, careful people always casting about to preserve their reputation and social standing never can bring about a reform. Those who are really in earnest must be willing to be anything or nothing in the world's estimation, publicly and privately, in season and out, avow their sympathy with despised and persecuted ideas and their advocates and bear the consequences." I'm not saying that you and I all need to become activists, but this statement got me thinking, "Being willing to become nothing." There may just lie in that statement the greatest culture rebellion of all, and I want to tell you about someone who lived like that and serves as my greatest inspiration.

I haven't mentioned much about my faith up to this point. I know there are a diverse group of people reading this book: those who share my Christian faith and those who, for whatever reasons, don't.

I don't want you to skip this part if you don't share my faith in Jesus. I want you to hear why I think He was probably the greatest culture rebel in history and why He's still interested in leading that movement. Whether you come from a background where you found yourself in Sunday school looking at a flannel-board version of Jesus and fooling around in class like I did, you come from a completely different faith, or you have had negative experiences with Jesus or those who claim to follow Him, humor me for a moment. Put away any fear that I'm trying to push my faith on you. I'm not. Throw away any preconceived visions of Jesus you've had. Put away the notion that I'm talking about Christianity or religion. I'm not. I want us to discover the person of Jesus and what made Him the most radical, revolutionary person who has ever changed history.

Jesus: The Ultimate Culture Rebel

Jesus was a normal guy just like you and me, other than the fact that He was supernaturally born through a virgin beside a pile of manure in a stable. (That part's a bit different.) Oh, and the fact that He's a deity. That's a bit different too. But the human side of Jesus was pretty normal. He grew up in a typical Jewish home, went through all the normal Jewish rituals and traditions, and became a carpenter like His dad. But Jesus thought and lived differently than those living in his time. His thoughts and values continue to be a complete reversal of the way every culture has thought since the beginning of the world; it is because of this that these thoughts are worth taking note of.

Jesus talked a lot about "the least of these." For someone leading a major spiritual movement, He didn't spend a lot of time schmoozing up to those in higher positions. In fact, He right out attacked the leaders of His day, calling them things like a "brood of vipers." Jesus clearly wasn't concerned with climbing the social ladder. Instead, He was found in the homes of people whom the culture despised and marginalized. He would hang out with prostitutes (can you imagine the rumors that started?), beggars, dishonest tax collectors whom everyone knew were stealing money, and unpopular fishermen who annoyed everyone with their "big talk" and anger issues. If this was happening today, we'd say Jesus was hanging out with a bunch of losers! He went further and officially called these people His disciples! He handpicked them to be on His team.

Popular culture, both then and now, subtlety instructs us to pick the best for our teams, leaving the weak to be picked last. (That was always me.) Jesus, however, reverses this unspoken rule and says that the weak are the strong ones. He radically teaches that the first will be last. He promises that those who are full of pride and high in their power positions will be brought lower, where their servants will rule over them.

That, friends, is completely the opposite of what we know as "normal." If our culture adopted those ideals, we would see some very different billboards: "Because your neighbor's worth it." "That employee deserves a break today." "Ba-da-da-da-da ... I'm loving you." These slogans only sound ridiculous because we're not used to hearing this reverse talk.

Jesus pushed people to their limits. He drove the religious leaders of His day nuts. Hate organized religion? Looks like Jesus did too. He challenged people's thinking by saying things like, "You have heard—" and then adding His radical theology by stating His, "But I say—" Here's an example of this: Jesus said, "You have heard, 'You shall not commit murder. Whoever commits this is to appear in court.' But I say to you then everyone who is angry with his brother is guilty before the court" (Matthew 5:21–2). Or how about this one?

"You have heard it was said, 'You shall not commit adultery,' but I say to you that everyone who *looks* at a woman to lust for her has already committed adultery with her already in his heart" (Matthew 5:27–8). Jesus cut straight past the outward layer that people tended to judge and went straight for the heart. He attacked anger and lust rather than the final acts of murder and adultery. No one in His time had ever heard anything like this. His radical theology blew some minds and drove others mad.

Jesus went as far to say, "If you grasp and cling to life on your terms, you'll lose it, but if you let that life go, you'll get life on God's terms" (Luke 17:33). Just knowing a little bit about Jesus doesn't cost you anything, but choosing to follow Him will cost you everything. You were born to find Him.

He Really Is Offensive

Everything Jesus said and stood for was extremely offensive, even to some of those who followed Him closely. When they weren't offended, they were dumbfounded, and they tried to figure out what on earth He meant. I remember when Jesus offended me. I had known Him for a long time. I was even working as a pastor! I was building a kingdom that He wasn't impressed with, but when He challenged my heart, I took offense. Instead of accepting His words, I stumbled over them and found myself in a dark place for a couple of years. All He was asking was for me to be willing to lose myself and my success (not a lot to ask, right?), and I refused. (Note to self: refusing God is a bad idea.) I got my way, but through a series of very unfortunate events, I realized that my way wasn't actually getting me anywhere. (Frank Sinatra was wrong.) This left my heart in ruins.

Jesus really offended a young man back in His generation. This young man was rich. Today, he may have pulled up in his Lamborghini dressed in Versace from top to bottom. He was the very image of success and was also morally set, meaning that he was not only rich but a good "church boy" who kept all the "rules." He had come to ask Jesus how to attain eternal life. Jesus commended him for all the great things he was doing but then said something that stopped this young man in his tracks: "One thing you lack … go sell everything and follow me" (Mark 10:21). Silence. Shock. Jesus couldn't be serious, could He? Jesus just told this young man to go and sell everything he owned. Surely, He didn't mean the car? Could he at least keep the Versace socks? The young man got back in his Lamborghini and drove away. (Okay, it was actually a camel.) He couldn't do it. The verse says that he went away, saddened. "When we say that we want to be His disciple, yet attach a list of conditions, Jesus refuses to accept our terms. His terms involve unconditional surrender" (Richard Stearns).

Jesus states, "What good is it for a man to gain the whole world, yet lose his soul" (Mark 8:34–6). We ask how much a man gives, and Jesus asks how much he keeps. Jesus may not be asking you and me to sell everything and live on the streets, but He *is* asking for us to be willing to give up our love of money. Even if your answer is a hesitant yes, then you are off to a great start. If we are open to the idea of giving Him our whole lives and asking Him to help us journey this road less travelled, He will come alongside us. But the hoarding heart will indeed be left to continue living a life of clutching stuff only to find that all the stuff can't be taken past death's door.

The more I relearn about who He is, the more He offends my selfish heart and reveals the true condition of my humanity. I can do nothing but bow in surrender, realizing that I truly do need a savior. He's not just someone I look to for purpose and meaning; He's someone I need. That's it. I'm undone. I must give Him my all, because His very character calls for all of me. And in my loss of life, He gives me His; now the true culture rebel living can start.

You need Christ in order to be a change agent because one day, good-karma thinking won't be enough to sustain the good you really desire to do. You'll get hurt and run over, and in yourself, you won't have the power to get back up. Nice people are nice, but "being nice" isn't good enough. Forgiven people can truly forgive, and transformed hearts bring transformation. You've got to have something more than your own strength.

I can hear Jesus calling to our generation: "Stop your altruism! Stop focusing on being nice. Stop thinking all of this will bring you good karma from the universe!" This thinking, although noble, is still based on the self. The way of the cross is selfless. It abandons all aspects of "what's in it for me." It doesn't look for that "warm, fuzzy feeling" you get from giving to the less fortunate. Jesus takes it further and asks who we are really giving for? How inconvenienced are you really willing to be? Can you give, even if it costs you? Jesus goes straight for our hearts and their motivations. Many of us are willing to give, *if* we can still have what we want. But what if giving means we give up the things we want? There, friends, is the narrow road set before us. Many choose to avoid it because it is difficult to give up the rights to yourself in order to embrace Him. Will you avoid it? Or are you curious to find out what happens if you dare to walk this path? You want to know where Jesus is? He's with the poor. It's time to go from being one who is blind to culture to becoming a culture rebel.

I can hardly wait another minute. The best part of the book is nearly among us. In order for you and I to have any hope of offering our families and those who surround us anything that is real and true, we have had to come face-to-face with what we were blinded by. I hope you've switched to the side of fighting against the status quo. There are injustices in our world we haven't seen. There are needs we didn't notice before that are now larger than life and staring straight at us. We now get to discover what they are and which ones *you* carry an answer to. This is exciting stuff!

Rebels for a Cause

"**I**n order to serve our world, we must betray it," Bono once said. I've always wanted to change the world. I'm inspired by stories of people who have left their fingerprints on the very face of culture. I want to be a historymaker. I want to be one who people remember as a person who revolutionized her world. As noble as this sounds, I'm afraid that up until a few years ago, this has come from a very self-serving motivation. I truly did want to love people and make a difference for their benefit, but I also wanted the credit. Visions of winning a Nobel Prize danced through my mind; dreams of becoming the "woman of the year." I've thought out speeches just in case. I can't believe I just admitted that to you. I must really like you.

I had to come to a broken place in order to be ready to bring about the change I so desired to initiate. You see, transformation, no matter how small or big, is never about us. It's not about the recognition we will receive or about the merit badge that will feed your need for approval. No, it's the most selfless thing we will ever do. We need to be trustworthy to lead such efforts.

All it takes is a heart that truly cares for others—that's it. Once your eyes are off yourself, you become incredibly useful! What a thrill it is to add benefit to others and get no credit for it. It makes you giddy like when you were a child hiding where no one else could find you. You know what that giddiness is called? Joy. And when you've got that kind of joy, no one can steal it. It's the real deal. It brings strength to your bones. Women who are in slavery to self-objectification rarely rise to be leaders and world-shakers—even though they carry this very DNA inside of them. Here lies the greatest rebellion of all—rebellion to *ourselves.*

Being a rebel for a cause will take a few more mental switches, switches such as these:

From Cluttered to "Holey"

Question: What are we cluttering our minds with? Your mind is like a closet. If we took a microscope into your mind, would we find it spacious and full of beneficial things in their perfect places or a chaotic mess filled with litter and garbage spilled everywhere?

You are being exploited by media, and you're doing nothing about it. Don't believe me? Open your eyes to the hundreds of ads you see on average each day. Apparently, your body is assisting the billion-dollar marketing industry of products that are only feeding our insecure, sexy-craving culture. We see this trend on a daily basis within the context that the media portrays women in, namely that we are meant to be viewed and that our value comes from how we look. It teaches men to view us as such as well. It subtly forms values we consider "normal." Values such as the following:

- A new wardrobe will make it all better!
- It's time to cover up the gray.
- Wouldn't it be nice to not be an A cup? There's an operation for that.
- Split ends are a dire situation that can be solved by "this" product.
- Flabby arms, legs, butts, and abs are never to be seen in public. Ever.

- Wrinkles equal "not sexy." Do whatever it takes to stay young-looking.

And we fall for it. In the film *Miss Representation*, they state, "In the world of a million channels, media tries to do more shocking things to break through the clutter through sometimes even violent, sexually offensive, and demeaning messages."

According to the film, the average teen spends thirty-one hours a week watching TV, seventeen hours listening to music (heard today's top forty lately?), three hours a week watching movies, four hours a week reading magazines (do you really think they mean *TIME Magazine*?), and ten hours a week online. I don't allow my family to watch *The Simpsons*. Okay, that sounds a bit severe. It's not that I don't "allow" them. I just frown on it. I tell them that the show steals brain cells, to which my hubby answers, "But it's hilarious!" There are many shows I think suck the brain cells right out of us: *The Hills, Jersey Shore, Desperate Housewives, South Park*, among many others. I can't begin to tell you how much I despise shows like that. Not only do I believe that they steal our brain cells, but I also believe that after they steal them, they replace them with ones that look and sound like their characters. And don't get me started on music and its power over the brain. I'm a dancer. I listen to lyrics because the words *and* the beat dictate my movement. You tell me to loosen up my buttons. Well, I just might.

If media isn't going to shape culture, what will? I have a crazy alternative to offer. What if the below defined women instead?

- Impressive character
- One whose husband trusts without a doubt to not sleep with every man on the block (and not to spend their life savings on Starbucks)
- One who speaks well of her husband—even in the midst of catty women complaining about their "useless" hubbies
- Inventiveness

- Creativity
- Hardworking
- Generous to the poor, embracing them rather than shunning them
- A good investor
- One who doesn't give in to mass consumption for herself but invests wisely, thinking about her family's future
- One whose family weathers financial storms just fine because she's smart with her money
- Someone you won't catch watching *The Real Housewives*
- Hardly lazy
- One who has great style that is bought without a credit card and shows her worth and dignity
- One who considers wisdom to be better than status
- One who embraces her age
- One who knows that beauty will fade
- One who cares to pattern her life after God and receives identity from Him instead of falling for the messages media tries to sell her

This woman described in Proverbs 31 is a picture of an outstanding role model for all us women, young and old. However, after they read the passage, most women say, "I could never live up to that kind of standard," and head off to try to measure up to the standards the media places on women's beauty and worth. Umm, okay ... but do you see how stupid that is, or is it just me?

I remember listening to a tape (yes, a tape) of Tony Campolo when I was sixteen. I listened to that tape so many times I had it memorized. One of the things he said on the tape referred to women and sin. It has never left me. Before the word "sin" makes you shudder with all the preconceived ideas that go along with it, bear with me. He stated that the Greek word for sin was *hamartia*, which means, "to miss the mark."

Interesting. It doesn't mean to break the rules. Here's what he stated about women after he this definition: "For a woman to not become all that she was meant to be is sin. She's missing the mark. When she dumbs herself down to not threaten the insecure male, she is forfeiting all that God created her for." It is my responsibility as a woman birthed for such a time as this to be a walking, living alternative for others to see. How are women to see we were made for so much more if we, too, are buying into all the junk and deception the media throws at us?

There's nothing like a good de-clutter session; I call this a "chuck fest." When we go through our house and throw out all our junk, we make room for new junk (well, at least that's how it seems to go). What's preferable is after a good chuck fest, there should be room to walk, breathe, and for anything useful to again be able to find its place. Sometimes we have to do the same thing with our minds in order for a new mindset to be able to take place. This has been referred to as "a renewing" (Romans 12:1).

Take some time to think about what you watch. Does it influence you? No, seriously, stop the justification and really think about how you behave. What about the music you listen to? What does it feed you? There was a time I had to make a switch from top-forty radio to our "family friendly" station because I realized I was becoming incredibly focused on being sexy. The word "sexy" was in over half the songs I was listening to, and I was living to bring sexy back. I didn't change stations out of any legalistic thinking. I did it because I value my mind and my heart and realized that whatever I let into my eyes and ears feeds my soul. I want my soul focused on what's eternal and real. "I'm Sexy and I Know It" is just too temporal for where I want my heart to be.

Time to get "holey," people! If I want to bring anything back, it's a commitment to holiness. I don't know what image of Hutterite-type living just entered your mind, but get it out right now. All that means is that I care about what God cares about. The reason I spelled it "holey," by the way, is because of a story I heard about a young man who took scissors and cut out every mention of wealth, loving the poor, and feeding the hungry out of his Bible. He stood in front of a crowd, showing his Bible full of holes. He then stated, "Brothers and sisters, this is our American Bible. It is full of holes. Each one of us might as well take our Bibles, a pair of scissors, and begin cutting out all the scriptures we pay no attention to." That got my attention.

In the book *The Hole in Our Gospel*, where I read the story I just described, the author, Richard Stearns, calls the gospel a "social revolution." But I can't even comprehend that, let alone be involved while I'm sitting there watching yet another one-night stand and wishing I looked more like Sarah Jessica Parker. Friends, it's time to wake up and get off the couch. It's time to perform a "chuck fest" on our souls.

From Numbness to a Broken Heart

No one wants their heart broken. When it's from a hurtful situation, it can send you into the depths of despair. When it's from the pain you see in the world, it's hard to know what to do with it. It's the strangest feeling to care for something, to want so badly to do something, but to have no blinkin' clue what to do.

After a good "chuck fest" and allowing your mind to be cleared from all the garbage, you will be able to see and process new things, things such as needs you never knew were in front of you. As "you" become less of a priority in your mind and others begin to take your place, you will be overwhelmed with how much need there is. And that's when it will happen: you will go through a "system overload" phase where everything seems to break your heart. You will be tempted to want to be an answer to everything you see, but you can't be. Resist the temptation to want to be the world's savior, but don't be afraid of the heartbreak; it's a good thing.

Compassion comes from the Latin words "with" and "suffering." When compassion starts to take root in your heart, you grow beyond a "grinch heart." Compassion takes the whole heart over. Your heart will "feel" again when you hear that half of the world's children are born into poverty, that there are approximately 150-170 million orphans around the globe, and that 70 percent of the world's poor are women and their children.

I remember when I read those stats in Jennifer Grant's book *Love You More*, which details her story of adopting her daughter from Guatemala. I finished the book in one day and cried like a baby through the whole thing. God was breaking my heart for the orphan. I can't imagine any child being alone and dying from hunger. For the first time in a long time, I felt something for someone other than myself.

Here's the problem with the heartbreak: it's hard to find what it is you have the answer to. There's no shortage of need. In fact, it's overwhelming. We can't imagine where we are going to find the time in our crazy schedules! Here's a crazy thought: maybe it's time for a schedule shift! I've recently done this. I'm known for being all over the place, but this fall, I got a little crazy and took a ton of activities *out* of my schedule, giving me room to include anything God may put on my lap. There were days I freed up time only to find myself with nothing to do. I used to be very uncomfortable with idle time, but it's given me room to play with my kids and read. On other days, He put random homeless people in my path, people to whom I would actually have time to talk.

It's a good thing my schedule cleared up, because the adventure God was setting up for me was going to require a lot of time. I began to call up organizations working to combat poverty in my city, asking if I could meet with them. Some weeks, I would meet with one organization a day *with* my kids in tow. Every time, I would leave the meeting with a greater understanding of the needs in my city and a burning passion to help. As a result, I have built relationships with over twenty organizations in my city and produced a hip-hop show raising funds for and awareness of poverty issues, highlighting the work of these organizations. I continue to work with them as well as

Calgary's Poverty Reduction Initiative. If I hadn't freed up my time, this could have never happened.

You may need to really look at how nuts your schedule is. Do you have room for a little inconvenience? If someone in need showed up in front of you today, would you have time for them? Or would you have to apologize repeatedly for leaving them in the ditch because of your son's scheduled soccer practice? Do you feel a nudge in your heart to let go of some things? It could be for a reason.

Because I believe in healthy activity and allowing my son to pursue his passions, he is allowed *one* activity, not three, not two, just one. I do that so we can keep life from becoming too complicated. Our schedules could be the very things that keep us from the needs around us. What feeds us this idea of a busy schedule? Our culture tells us that busy equals productive and that programs are good for your kids so that they can stay out of trouble. I think my son loves being with me making sandwiches for our "Brown Baggin' It" lunch program at the local school better than he likes his gymnastics program. Just sayin'. "And inconvenience is an adventure wrongly considered" (G. K. Chesterton).

Detox and Revolutionize

Have you ever tried going off sugar for a month? I'm one of those crazy people who love detoxing. The hardest thing to do is to give up sugar, however. I never knew that it was in *everything* until I committed to giving it up for a month! The first day was killer. Actually, the first *week* was killer. Was I ever grumpy! My poor family. I'm sure that every time the word "detox" comes out of my mouth, my hubby wants to run away with the kids to a hotel. It's not fun. If you've tried it, you get it. If you haven't, try it. I dare you, but first plan your husband and children's trip away.

There are so many benefits of detoxing. However, the process is horrific. I'm detoxing right now as I write this book so I can have clarity of mind. Can I quickly ask, "Why on earth did I choose Starbucks as my location of writing then?" Those baked treats are screaming my name right now. You may be able to hear the blueberry bar calling me through the pages. This is torture; however, I must type, and for heaven's sake, I should stop talking about those baked goods!

Once the body is cleansed from all the harmful things I put into it and expose it to, it can function more efficiently. As you allow your mind to be renewed with a new way of thinking and see the world through new eyes, you will need to continually detox yourself from the world's thinking. That's a hard thing to do, because like sugar, culture has a powerful message that just happens to be *everywhere*, even on cereal boxes.

Because we can't (and shouldn't) resort to running to live in the mountains away from all influences of society, we need to create a discipline of feeding our soul things that will continue to stir in us the heart of a culture rebel. For too long, we have allowed the surrounding pop culture to disciple us. We need to be disciplined by something of meaning and essence; I can't think of anything better than the Bible.

Did I just scare you? Would it make you feel better to know that most people, Christians included, struggle with reading it? The Bible is probably the only book that occupies most shelves in homes all over North America but is rarely opened. It's a bit intimidating. Where do you start? It's so flippin' huge, and there are a lot of words and phrases that are hard to understand. How do you "read" the Bible? I mean, do you just bunker down for a week and try to get the whole thing read cover to cover?

If you're sweating, just relax. I'm going to give you some super Bible-reading tips, but first, let me tell you why this is the book for you to read in order to keep yourself detoxed and culture rebel-ready.

As we saw in the previous chapters, Jesus' thoughts and teachings are completely counterculture. The only way to learn something is through repetition. You could play "Name That Tune" with TV ads, and we'd all jump to say the answer. How do we know them? By hearing them all the time.

My son, who's five at present, just learned the version of "Jingle Bells" with "Batman smells" (you instantly thought of the next line, didn't you?) through some crazy kid who taught him using this repetition method (bless that child). Now my son is using repetition to drive his mother nuts by singing this over and over again at home.

What we value, we become. If we value The Pussycat Dolls, all it takes is a little repetition, and *bam*, we've adopted their frame of reference. I think you get the picture. So, if we've been challenged by Jesus and think His teachings are the radical spark plug and we want to boost ourselves into some holy rebellion, then perhaps a little repetition is needed. Because He's not going to show up on your doorstep, it's a good thing He had some people write all His thoughts down, isn't it? Here's an easy guide to reading your Bible:

How to Read the Bible for People Who Don't Read the Bible Good (inspired by Zoolander)

- Start with a good Swiffer to dust it off (or better yet, purchase an updated version that uses today's English). The Message is a great version that uses today's language.
- Next, open it up to Matthew. There's amazing stuff in the first half (the Old Testament), but let's start with Jesus' teachings and get more in-depth later.
- Read one chapter a day. Start with a coffee in hand, a pen, and a journal. Then as you read through carefully, ask yourself the following questions: "What is this saying to me? Why was this written? Who is being spoken of or to? Where is this taking place? How do I relate? Can I see anything I can apply to my life at this moment?" Write all your answers down in the journal. Don't just speed read; think about it. Let it challenge you. How is what Jesus saying different than the messages delivered daily by our surrounding culture? How is it different than your normal way of thinking? Ask God to help you understand what you're reading. He's thrilled you're reading. Of course He wants to help!
- Join a group that is studying the Bible. Don't know of anyone? Do some searching around for those who may be interested and start your own group.

- Don't read what you want to hear. Read what is being said. If you value Jesus' words more than anything, they will change your life. Wait no longer. Put this book down and pull out the book that will truly change your life. Your Bible exploration starts today.

The "Revolutionize" Part

People who know God will be strong and do mighty exploits. That was written to a brave young man named Daniel, another culture rebel who refused to worship the gods of his culture and stayed true to his God. He was willing to be thrown to a bunch of hungry lions because of his faith, but God spared his life. Thank goodness we're not "thrown to lions" today for our rebellion to our own culture's religion. It's a good thing, because we have a hard enough time standing out as it is. It's much easier to go with the flow than to be the revolutionary person Jesus inspires us to be, but it's not half as much fun.

Every day, injustice, poverty, and corruption cloud the face of God in our current culture. You steward an answer. There are over two thousand verses in the Bible that talk about poverty and injustice. It's time for us to pay attention to them. When God is defaced, the human race is defaced. It's time for our rebellion to turn revolutionary. Bono, fighting for those dying of AIDS, challenges us with this: "We can be the generation that no longer accepts that an accident of latitude determines whether a child lives or dies ... but will we be that generation? History will be our judge, but what's written is up to us. We can't say our generation didn't know how to do it. We can't say our generation couldn't afford it. And we can't say our generation didn't have reason to do it. It's up to us. It's not about charity; it's about justice."

God is passionate about justice. There are acts of injustice all over: bullying, racism, poverty, corruption, greed, love of money, drug culture, human trafficking, just to name a few. We need to burn with discontent and let that burning move us to action. Change only happens when someone gets sick of the status quo. Our world and all that it's become is what it is because of what we've put up with. We've put up with some real garbage, and it's time for rebellion! Confucius said, "To know what is right and not do it is the worst cowardice." Are you up for taking your place in God's social revolution? You were made for this. You were born for this time. "In the end, we will remember not the words of our enemies, but the silence of our friends" (Martin Luther King). It's time to speak what's burning in your heart. It's time to see what God has placed in you as an answer. Dare to find it. Dare to do it.

"Sometimes I would like to ask God why He allows poverty, suffering and injustice when He could do something about it, but then I'm afraid He might ask me the same question." —anonymous

From Culture Rebel to Culture Maker

You were born to *make* culture. Being a culture rebel isn't the end; it's the beginning. It's the wake-up call that allows you to see what you've been falling for. It stirs questions that turn into revelations of what "could be" instead of what we have complacently accepted in the past. You may wonder how you, in your seemingly ordinary life, can shape culture. Sit back and grab another cup of homemade coffee because I'm about to show you how.

In his brilliant book *Culture Making*, Andy Crouch describes "culture" as what humans make of the world. Inside of us, there is a desire to make something beautiful. You see it in children as they create on paper an imagined world they've created in their minds. As children, we dreamed of what could be; we imagined clouds made of marshmallows and houses made of chocolate. That same spirit to make the world better is still there inside us, buried by the weight of responsibility and anguish from harsh life experiences. To some, the idea of changing the world sounds idealistic and foolish; they don't want to leave their comfortable state to dream only to find it all crash down on them. None of us want to fail. We don't want to look stupid.

You have two options: You can continue to live buried under what reality the world has created for you, never knowing what you were truly capable of, or you can take a risk. Normal people continue to produce more normal, status-quo types of people. You can choose to step out, fail, learn, step out again, and possibly see something beautiful that wasn't there before become a tangible reality for you and those around you. "Are you confident enough to encourage people to do what's right, useful, and joyful, as opposed to what the system has always told them to do?" (Seth Godin)

Change Your World

I have had numerous conversations with women in particular about "changing the world." The concept always seems to freak them out. It's not that they don't want to. They just don't know how. The "how" is too overwhelming to the mom with two young kids under five. That woman isn't in a world-changing mindset; she's in survival mode. When her eyes glaze over and start looking at me like I'm speaking in a foreign language, I go chat with a young adult about this concept and watch their idealistic eyes enlarge.

This idea of "changing the world" is a rather new concept to our time in history. Of the 1.5 million titles in Harvard's collections published before 1900, *zero* included references to changing the world. But the amount of Google searches for "changing the world" in 2007 was 8,770,000 (Andy Crouch, *Culture Making*). Apparently, changing the world has become a popular concept, an overwhelming one at that.

Whether you are one of those moms living in survival mode or you are a young adult who still believes in marshmallow clouds, I'm happy to say that changing the world is doable for you. I want to take the pressure off your shoulders right now by telling you the truth: you *cannot* change the world. Uh-oh. My young adult friend's marshmallows just melted. The survival mom stopped to look up.

You can't change the world, but you *can* change *your* world—the world you presently live in, the street you live on, the school you or your kids go to, the place you work, your home. Those you can influence. And you know what? It's significant. To all the "Connie-type," overachieving dreamers reading, I know what I just told you will not be enough. I know for you, if it doesn't involve stadium-sized impact, it's just not big enough. I would like to tell you what that still small voice told me not too long ago: "Get over yourself." Stop trying to impact the orphans in Africa, the human trafficking in Europe, and those who are working in factories in China while you don't even know the family who lives next door to you. (I know. It hurt me to hear that too.)

Maybe one day us overachievers will have an impact on people on a completely different continent. Maybe you will one day find yourself leading a stadium-sized movement, but while you're waiting for these great opportunities to arise, may I offer the humble idea of meeting your neighbors? Why not invite them over for dinner and get to know them? Share your sugar. Look for needs in your own community. Find out what you can offer to the city you live in. Research the growing number of working poor in your city and see what you can do can do about that. Volunteer to make lunches for kids who go to the local school, haven't had breakfast, and have no lunch either. It's a humble beginning, but world domination is right around the corner, I'm sure.

Truth is that everyone has the capacity for creating change. "Everyone" includes those who feel competent and those who feel powerless. It includes the businessman, the mom with a coffee IV attached to her arm, the idealistic young adult, and the innocent child.

Act Small in a Big Way

Did you know that Van Gogh only sold one painting in his lifetime? I was surprised to learn this, as I thought that he was always a big-time artist, even while he was alive. I mean, he's now got his own Baby Einstein DVD. He created something the world appreciated. It wasn't great in quantity, but its quality made the world take notice.

There is something to be said about quality. We don't truly know its value in a world of mass production. There's something about a handwritten card that triumphs the store-bought version. There's something special about an original painting as opposed to a copy. People value something that has been made from scratch by loving hands. Take lasagna, for example. Who doesn't want to sink their teeth into that homemade masterpiece?

When you go "big," sometimes people go home. There's a shift even in the business world to focus on "tribes" rather than masses of public. Tribes are smaller groups of people who are passionate about the same things you are. Companies are catching on that people are slowly making this shift in value. Though we may still stop at the massive "Stuff Mart" for prices we're forced to afford, we value and are choosing to pass its doors to give the local business full of homemade goodness our allegiance.

"If you persist in trying to be all things to all people, you will fail. The only alternative then is to be something important to a few people. To get there, you must disappoint some slightly engaged normal people who can probably live just fine without you," Seth Godin once said.

Don't sit there because you feel you can't do something big. You can still do *something*. Small is enough. Somewhere, our human race became fixated with "bigness." Simultaneously, it has also increased the size of our heads. Helen Lee says in her book *The Missional Mom*, "Think big and act small." This paradox is just the remedy needed to shrink ourselves back to a reality that needs what we have.

The culture we see in play before our eyes right now started small. Someone somewhere got an idea and started to implement it. They found others who believed in the same things, and together, they shaped what we are presently experiencing. Who says that can't be you and me making the culture that Jesus has envisioned for the world (the "world" meaning the street you live on).

The Ripple Experiment

Take a quick minute and get a glass of water. Don't worry, I'll wait. I'll just catch a very interesting conversation behind me that I can listen in on while you're gone.

You're quick! Okay, now take your finger, dip it in the water, and lift your finger above the glass. Allow a drop to fall into the water. What does it do? It sends little waves out to the side of the glass, doesn't it? If you didn't think it was fascinating enough, grab something bigger … like a bowl or the bathtub! Get your kids doing this too! Free fun for all!

I'm no scientist, but I can make a couple of observations. First, a small drop ripples. It doesn't matter if it's the smallest drop of rain into a puddle or a giant piece of hail falling into a pond. *All* drops cause ripples. Secondly, the size of the object holding the water determines how far the ripple goes. I sure hope my grade-six science teacher reads this book. She would be so proud.

The ripple experiment demonstrates an important truth: we can each have an impact on our world, no matter how big or small. We've covered that already. What we need to observe for our lives is that the wider our reach, the bigger the impact. What does this mean? It means that the farther your hands reach, the more impact you will have. That means you have to take your hands out of your pockets and reach them out wide in front of you. Before you go walking around with your arms extended out at shoulder level and scaring all those who pass you on the street, I think you know that I'm not talking about your physical arms. I'm talking about your heart. Living with a big heart that isn't afraid of reaching into places and people that may be out of your comfort zone determines the size of your influence.

One more observation: Get a buddy or your kids to drip water from your fingers into the same water source. Notice how the ripples got bigger because of the greater depth of impact? A small group of people can do some crazy things. A small group of people, each person with his or her own focused heart, can make greater waves than just my one drip. Looks like we'll need some buddies.

Why not find some crazy friends to make some culture with you? Anything's more fun with someone else! I have a crazy buddy who found out about this ministry in Las Vegas that ministers to prostitutes called "Hookers for Jesus." We always joke about doing something like that (not the hooking part). It's our code when we're thinking of something crazy to do—Code: H4J. We all need H4J types of people in our lives. They're hard to find, but you'll find them. Once you step out, they'll often find you. If not, you can always resort to bribing your friends to come along with you in return for your secret sauce recipe. "Never doubt that a small group of thoughtful, committed citizens can change the world; indeed, it's the only thing that ever has" (Margret Mead).

Create!

We have reached the conclusion of the book. What a journey we have had! I'm still in Starbucks. I often wonder what life was like before Starbucks. I was alive at the time, but I can't seem to imagine the world without it now that it has taken over the entire coffee empire. (I apologize to my Canadian fans of Tim Hortons. Admit defeat.)

Starbucks president Howard Shultz had a vision of an experience of coffee he wanted to create for people. He didn't want a coffee shop where people would just come in, get their coffee, and leave. Inspired by coffee shops in Milan, he turned the company into an experience rather than just a place to buy coffee beans. We now willingly pay five dollars a latte for that experience.

We can see how Howard Shultz created culture in Seattle. He didn't set out to change the world, just that one store on the Pike Place Harbor. But the world noticed, and now there is a Starbucks in more than fifty-five countries. They presently have 18,887 stores worldwide, many of which are across the street from one another. You could say Howard Shultz has done his share of culture-making. Remember this the next time you say, "Wanna go get a Starbucks?" instead of saying just "coffee."

That same culture-making potential is held in your hands. What will you do with the cultural power you have? Stop doubting you have it. We are furnishing heaven with what we bring to God's earth. There's a blank canvas in front of you. What picture will you paint? For those of us who can offer no more than stick men, what are we doing presently that will add to the architecture of heaven? For me, my writing and my dance company are tiny offerings I offer as a gift to the earth. My money and time are also small contributions. "Culture is not changed simply by thinking: the only way to change culture is to make more of it" said Andy Crouch..

Offer your alternative. You have something our world is in desperate need of. You are called to cultivate. See what is around you, and then look for what is lacking. What can you offer our world? I'm sorry. I can't answer this specifically for you. You'll have to do some digging for yourself. For ideas on what this looks like, check out the Culture Rebel blog where I share stories of people making culture in their world. Read the book *Small Things with Big Love* by Margot Starbuck (no relation to Starbucks), which is what I call the perfect how-to-create-culture-for-the-clueless guide. Read the list of my culture rebels at the back, and let their stories inspire you. "Business as usual" is done. It's time for you to embrace the call of a culture rebel who makes culture. I believe you can.

"Derive your identity not from what you consume, but what you create" —Andy Crouch

Culture Rebels

These culture rebels are in no particular order of "importance," only alphabetical to show that it doesn't matter if you're leading a multibillion-dollar industry or just inviting your neighbor over for dinner. All efforts to live outside of ourselves are significant and useful. *That* in itself is a mindset that deserves rebellion. In this list, you'll see "big" right next to "smaller," but we know that in the end, making culture can't be measured. (Some of the people mentioned in this list were authors mentioned in the book but are indeed culture rebels as well.)

LeeAnne Alexander and Alexis Harrison
Help neighbors in need through a network of community volunteers and donors expressing concern for their neighbors in practical ways through "Neighbourlink."
www.neighbourlinkcalgary.ca

Jenny Rae Armstrong
Jenny writes about the pressing issues surrounding women. She's not afraid to tackle the hard stuff!
www.jennyraearmstrong.com

Matthew Barnett
Founder of the LA Dream Centre. Author of *The Cause within You.*
www.dreamcenter.org

Karen Beattie
Karen writes about faith, culture, and the search for abundance at
www.karenbeattie.net

Amy Julia Truesdell Becker
Author of *A Good and Perfect Gift*, which is about her journey of
having her daughter, Penny, who has Down syndrome.
www.amyjuliabecker.com

Lisa Bevere
Author of the book *Nurture.*
www.messengerinternational.org

Tracey Truhlar Bianchi
Author of *Green Mama: The Guilt-Free Guide of Helping You and Your
Kids Save the Planet.* Check out her blog at www.traceybianchi.com

Amy Wolgemuth Bordoni
Any writes about life, real issues, and inspirations.
www.dontstampthebaby.blogspot.ca

Vicky Burke
One of my mentors growing up, Vicky has given her life to serve the
marginalized in Toronto. Words can't express my respect for her.

Dawn Bury of Birthday Buddies
Women who saw the need for children living in shelters (as a result
of their fleeing domestic violence) to have a birthday party. These
women bring the party to them!
www.birthdaybuddies.ca

Valerie Cade
Valerie comes alongside those who are experiencing bullying in their workplace and gives them the tools to overcome.
www.BullyFreeatWork.com

Suanne Ashcroft Camfield
A freelance writer, speaker, and editor. She is the blog manager for Fulfill, a nonprofit effort focused on mobilizing women to invest their influence in the world for God's purposes. www.suannecamfield.wordpress.com

Francis Chan
Author of *Crazy Love*.
www.francischan.org

Jenn Co
Jenn acts as the resident treasure hunter and scours the city for all these great finds. If it's inspiring, hope-filled and downright fun, she's sure to uncover it.
www.anythingbrilliant.com

Elisabeth Klein Coran
Beth is a refreshing for anyone who has been through a divorce and all the struggles it entails.
www.elisabethcorcoran.com

Andy Crouch
Author of *Culture Making*.
www.culturemaking.com

Sara Curdie
Advocate for broken women, women who are oppressed, victims of human trafficking. Brave enough to start a shelter for vulnerable women in Calgary.

My neighbor, Dawn
Dawn takes care of my kids when I'm stuck, and she gives me incredible advice on parenting my sons. She truly is the definition of a culture rebel who takes time to love her neighbors.

Ellen Painter Dollar
A writer focusing on faith, family, disability, and ethics, she is the author of *No Easy Choice: A Story of Disability, Parenthood, and Faith in an Age of Advanced Reproduction.*
www.ellenpainterdollar.com

Judy Douglass
Author of *Secrets of Success: Letters to My Children* and *Loving a Prodigal: Learning to Rest.* (Get the free e-book off her website.) A spunky woman who loves to encourage others to believe God for what He wants to do in and through them.
www.inkindle.wordpress.com

Lesa Shackelford Engelthaler
Lesa leads a movement for women in Texas, and every year, she takes a dozen or so women from Texas to love on, play with, tell our stories to, and hear the courageous stories of the women and girls at the House of Hope in Managua, Nicaragua.
www.houseofhopenicaragua.com

Janica Fisher
Janica works with "Humanity in Practice," which provides opportunities for people to make a difference in their community. From activities that involve parents and their children to school projects, HIP connects people to the "how" to engage in their city.
www.behip.ca

Seth Godin
Author of an amazing blog and the new book *We Are All Weird.*
www.sethgodin.typepad.com

Jennifer Grant
Author of *Love You More: The Divine Surprise of Adopting My Daughter*. Find out how she has embraced the orphan with her home at www.jennifergrant.com.

Marlena Proper-Graves
Marlena is making culture by painting pictures with words.
www.hispaththroughthewilderness.blogspot.ca

Ilona Hadinger
Ilona gives her life away by doing missions.
www.inkyspot.wordpress.com

Karin Henderson
Karin started a fitness group in her community that has brought more than fitness but true community among families who now know their neighbors.
www.facebook.com/Chapacisers/info

Rheanna Houston
A university student started a business called Carino that sells handmade products from women in Bolivia.
www.facebook.com/CarinoCreations

Allan Hirsch
Author of many books, such as *Untamed* and *The Faith of Leap*. Activist, dreamer, and one of the most Christ-like people you'll ever meet.
www.theforgottenways.org

Kerri Wyatt Kent
Author of many books that bring rest to the soul. Rest in a chaotic world? What a culture rebel she is!
www.keriwyattkent.com

Shelley Hunt
Started "Because I Can," which saves lives through encouraging organ donation.
www.facebook.com/pages/Because-I-Can-Project/306379722785083

Taryn R. Hutchinson
Author of *We Wait You: Waiting on God in Eastern Europe*, the real-life story of hearts transformed after the 1989 revolutions that forever changed Eastern Europe, as told by one woman who made a difference.
www.tarynhutchison.com

Claire Iffla
A force to be reckoned with. Justice advocate. Worshipper. Longtime friend.

Marilou Inkster
Marilou had the courage to dream of a big storehouse where practical needs could be met. She and her husband, Neil, provide eyeglasses to those who can't afford them.

Julie Jung-Kim
Julie provides a place for moms to be inspired and encouraged as they embrace their calling as mothers.
www.morethanjustmama.wordpress.com

Lara Krupicka
Lara inspires moms to bring ideals and actions into harmony.
www.larakrupicka.com

Terri Kraus
Terri writes passionately inspirational fiction.
www.terrikraus.com

Celina Laforet
The resource development manager of Sonshine Community Services, which provides shelter and counseling to women and children fleeing domestic violence.
www.sonshine.ab.ca

Steph Lambert
Steph started Justice ACTs, a Christian not-for-profit combating modern slavery through awareness programs in New Zealand, an organization whose aim is to seek, save, and restore those in slavery and being exploited.
www.justiceacts.org.nz

Helen Lee
Author of *The Missional Mom: Living with Purpose at Home and in the World*. Find out how she is changing her world at www.themissionalmom.com.

The girls from Legacy One (and the guys too)
Through dance, they influence the youth of today so that they use their gifts to live for a positive legacy.
www.legacyone.ca

Val Leiske
Founder of Fire Exit Theatre, a community theater company whose aim is to artistically explore the world with hope as a focus to challenge viewers to make choices to change.
www.fireexit.ca

Anita Lustrea
Host of the radio talk show *Midday Connection* (Moody Radio) and an artist. She is encouraging and thought-provoking.
www.anitalustrea.com

Vivian Mabuni
An Asian-American wife, mom, and cancer survivor. Vivian is currently writing a book on her journey through cancer. She's a brave soul.
www.vivianmabuni.com

Janelle Maclachlan
A young adult who serves at a local homeless shelter. She even chose to live homeless for a week to truly understand what the homeless she serves go through.

Tere Mahoney
Tere is working to reduce poverty in Calgary, Alberta. Activist, mom, perfect definition of "beautiful."
www.enoughforall.ca

Marika
CEO, recording artist, songwriter, producer, Marika manages a company that encourages, empowers, and equips artists in the entertainment industry.
www.emertonrecords.com

Kendra Melanson
One of the coolest B-girls I know who is impacting young people through dance and a life-changing message.
www.gxcanada.ca

Sheli Geoghan-Massie
Sheli lives in an inner-city neighborhood of Aurora, and she is a light to the community she lives in. Her family of six will be adding an addition of a little boy from Africa this summer. Her heart is warm and open for all.
www.shelimassie.blogspot.ca

Sharon Hodde Miller
Sharon encourages women to worship with their whole being.
www.sheworships.com

Marlene Molewyk
Marlene has an amazing story. Her career has included work as a broadcast journalist for an NBC affiliate and a production assistant for *The Oprah Winfrey Show*. A book is in the making!
www.marlenemolewyk.blogspot.ca

Shayne Moore
Author of *Global Soccer Mom: Changing the World Is Easier than You Think*. Find out about all she does with ONE Moms at www.shaynemoore.com.

Belinda Morrison
A local fitness boot camp owner who has a program of organizing boot camps for volunteer hours at community organizations.
www.bemorefitness.com

Alison Strobel Morrow
Alison writes beautiful fiction that inspires. Her current book is *Composing Amelia*.
www.alisonstrobel.com

Trillia Newbell
Trillia is setting a new standard in fitness, empowering women, and advocating racial equality.
www.trillfitnessonline.com

Enuma Okoro
Her book *Reluctant Pilgrim* talks about her search for deep community.
www.enumaokoro.com

Ruth Bell Olson
Ruth just brought home a baby boy from South Africa. Read about her journey at www.wheremybabiescomefrom.blogspot.ca.

Margaret Philbrick
Margaret is author, gardener, and teacher.
www.margaretphilbrick.com

Karen Swallow Prior
Associate professor of English and chair of the English and modern languages department at Liberty University in Lynchburg, Virginia. Read her thought-provoking and edgy articles on www.blog.christianitytoday.com/women.

Trina Pockett
Trina is a cancer survivor, a spitfire, and an igniter of women.
www.trinapockett.com

Tanya Power
Tanya is working to solve local child hunger through Brown Baggin' It for Kids.
www.brownbaggingit.org

Karen Reed
Shaping (v. sharing) a community of welcome in East Vancouver, opening her home to those in the community and offering radical hospitality.
karen.parkerhouse@gmail.com

Stephanie Kriegbaum Richer
Stephanie is honest and beautifully vulnerable. She embraces all. When I think of how open she is, I think of the heart of a culture rebel.
www.stephanierichter.blogspot.com

Caryn Dahlstrand Rivadeneira
Author of *Grumble Hallelujah*, which is about a woman who has learned joy through the grumbles. Check her out at www.carynrivadeneira.com.

Natasha Robinson
Natasha is big into mentoring women in leadership. Check out her blog.
www.sistasjourney.com

Sandy Rosen
Director of Mirror Dance Company, a unique, comprehensive training course for young adults who want to train toward a professional dance level with the goal of combining faith and art.
www.mirrordance.ca

Melinda Correa Schmidt
Radio host of *Midday Connection* (Moody Radio).
www.middayconnection

Karen Halvorsen Schreck
Author of *While He Was Away*, a tender and honest examination of love, longing, and loyalty in the face of modern war.
www.karenschreck.com/blog

Monica Robbins Selby
Monica writes passionately from her heart.
www.inthewhisper.com

Zahra Sharab
Director of Dikaios, Zahra produced a powerful show about human trafficking.

Amy Simpson
Editor of *Gifted for Leadership for Christianity Today*, Amy brings concepts to life with her words.
www.amysimpsononline.com

Alison Springer
Inspiring teen greatness in youth between the ages of twelve to twenty-four, Alison is building a generation of confident youth who will make positive choices that will shape and change their world. She is the founder of the Young Women of Power Conference.
www.inspiringteengreatness.com

Harriet Stanley
Harriet furnishes heaven with her art.
www.harrietstanley.com

Margot Starbuck
Author of Small *Things with Great Love: Adventures in Loving your Neighbour* and *Untamed*, this woman is witty and brilliant. Find out all her dynamic ideas and view Monday Minutes with Margot at www.margotstarbuck.com

Karen Sudds
Owner of Crossings Dance Ministries, Karen is making culture through expressions of dance by being in the community and creating sacred space.
www.crossingsdance.com

Arloa Sutter
Author of *The Invisible* and the founder of Breakthrough Urban Ministries, a ministry to the homeless in downtown Chicago.
www.arloasutter.com
www.breakthrough.org

Kristy-Anne Swart
Kristy-Anne is creating beauty and memories.
www.upandawaystudios.com

Susan Tam
Susan leads an initiative called "Transform Your Community," which is run out of her church, Midpark in Calgary, an initiative that engages their community in conversation that will make their community vibrant.
www.facebook.com/pages/Transform-Our-Community/19765708
0260306?sk=info

Kelli Blahnik Trujillo
Kelli is doing what she can for the environment.
www.kellitrujillo.com

Michelle Van Loon
Michelle tells the stories of spiritual ragamuffins and rebels.
www.michellevanloon.com

Beth McLean Wiest
Director of the choir "Harmony through Harmony," she gives voices for the voiceless and uses music to inspire justice.
www.youtube.com/watch?v=ewzqcdEd0K4

Renee Quinn and Alexandra Velosa
These women started "Role Mothers" out of Market Mall in Calgary, a program that they now manage, one inspiring women to not just shop but be role models for their families who can give back to the community.
www.rolemothers.ca

Sue Wells
Sue teaches cooking skills to kids in need. You don't need a website to start a nonprofit and do this.

Angie Cramer Weszley
Angie is the president of Caris Pregnancy Counseling and Resources.
www.caris.org

Melissa Wilson
Melissa is a university student who takes time out of her week to make bagged lunches for kids who don't have a lunch at a local middle school.

Karen Yates
Karen loves to talk about orphans, missions, and culture.
www.kareneyates.com

Kimberly McOwen Yim
Kimberly shares her own journey and what she and four of her friends are doing in their local community to educate and raise the engagement of the ordinary person in the fight against human trafficking.
www.abolitionistmama.blogspot.ca

Many names could have been added to this list. Women all over North America are rising up against the negative messages that the media imposes and are becoming women who make vibrant, meaningful culture around them! So whether you're doing it already or not, put your name down! If you're not yet making the culture you know you were born to make, write your name down as a commitment to it and see it through. Then e-mail me at culturerebelonline@gmail.com to tell me about it! I'd love to feature you on the Culture Rebel blog.

Your signature: _____

Rebel Resources

1. View the film *Miss Representation*, which can be bought or rented on iTunes. Viewer discretion is advised, but it is a powerful film about how media is influencing us today. www.missrepresentation.or

2. View the trailer for *Something to Say: Where Humanity Is Defaced*, which discusses poverty in a whole new way. www.youtube.com/watch?v=e8di7vjODuQ

3. *Story of Stuff* challenges viewers to put down their credit cards and start building a better world. www.storyofstuff.com

4. See the Global Rich List. You're richer than you think. www.globalrichlist.com

5. Redbud Writers Guild fearlessly expands the feminine voice in our churches, community, and culture. www.redbudwritersguild.com

6. *TED Talk* by Becky Blanton: "The year I was homeless." www.youtube.com/watch?v=KvvjDOtS2sw

7. The Real Housewives of West Vancouver is an amazing story.
www.canada.com/vancouversun/news/westcoastnews/story.html?id=bac0dce3-afff-409a-9a47-111663e6736a

8. Read this Red Letter article about what our sex-crazed culture is doing to women.
www.redletterchristians.org/patriarchy-pop-culture-and-pornography/

9. The city who ended hunger!
www.yesmagazine.org/issues/food-for-everyone/the-city-that-ended-hunger

10. Learn about a coffee shop that is making a difference.
www.youtube.com/watch?&v=wzdez9_f0G4

11. Don't hate me because I'm not a shoe person.
www.youtube.com/watch?v=5KkVbhA0zDM

12. Learn about the high price of materialism.
www.youtube.com/watch?v=oGab38pKscw&feature=youtu.be

13. *This* is what you need to look your hottest.
www.youtube.com/watch?v=lb1GEIBirBI&context=C3f03961ADOEgsToPDskJOOE7TnQq3zz1YhJYQ19RN

14. Watch Brene Brown's *TED talk* on vulnerability.
www.ted.com/talks/brene_brown_on_vulnerability.html

15. How you see can change how you act!
    www.youtube.com/watch?v=D38S9o_6qnc&featu
    re=youtu.be

16. Check out Culture Rebel on Facebook.
    www.facebook.com/pages/Culture-
    Rebel/264336430251705